Tafero's Lesson Plan of the Day - Intro to Business 101 - Banking and Financial Statements 1

Lesson One – General Business Terms

1. Be prepared to understand banks and financial statements
a. Analyze Annual Reports
b. Analyze Quarterly Reports
c. Analyze Monthly Statement
d. Analyze Balance Sheets
e. Analyze Market Share Charts
f. Analyze Sales Charts
g. Analyze Stock Charts

2. Risk vs Reward - what may be lost in relation to what may be gained

3. Business 4-activities that provide goods and services for a profit
4. Profit4 – assets-liabilities
5. Entrepreneur4 – person who risks time and money for profits
6. Revenue 5 – total sales
7. Loss 5 – when liabilities exceed assets
8. Risk5 – the chance you take in business to make a profit
9. Standard of living 5 – amount of goods and services you can afford
10. Quality of life 6 – political freedom, clean environment, education, health, safety, job satisfaction and free time

11. Stakeholders6 – illustrate on board
a. Stockholders
b. Customers
c. Community
d. Environment
e. Retailers
f. Employees
g. Government
h. Suppliers
i. bankers
12. Non-profit organization7 – organizations funded by donations that do not make profits
13. Factors of Production10-illustrate on board
a. Land (natural resources)
b. Labor
c. Capital
d. Ownership
e. Knowledge
14. Business environment12-illustrate on board
a. Economic
b. Legal
c. Technical
d. Competition
e. Social rules
f. Global conditions

15. Technology – 15 – machines and software
16. Productivity -15 – see Taylor – net profit in relation to time and work – give example 2 men
17. Ecommerce -16 – buying and selling goods and services online (then go over variables)
a. Less initial investment
b. Low transaction cost
c. Large purchases per transaction
d. Make more information available (business process)
e. Larger catalogs than real life print books
f. Flexibility
g. Improved customer interactions

18. Database -17 – Use ESD as an example on board – electronic storage of information
19. Empowerment20 –
a .responsibility
b. authority
c. freedom
d. training
e. equipment
20. Demography21 – human population size, density, age, race, gender and income (targeting ads)
21. Single Parent effect24 – targeted for TIME
22. Goods25 – things you can touch to buy
23. Services26 see chart on p27 – things you can't touch that you buy

Answer the following essay questions for homework
1. How should we assess potential profit against the possibility of loss (risk)? (1 par)
2. How has technology affected the business environment? (1 par)
3. How should we deal with our competition? (1 par)
4. Discuss global competition. (1 par)

Internet Resources For Homework:

General References

http://www.askmrmovies.com

Risk Assessment

www.deloitte.com

Tech in Business

www.businessweek.com/technology/

Competition in Business

Tafero's Lesson Plan of Day - Introduction to Business 101 - Competing in Global Markets - Two

Lesson 2 - Competing in Global Markets

What do we need to know in order to be able to compete globally? – What plays in NY does not necessarily play in Beijing. That goes for business as well as music.

Let us first look at one of the leading business lecturers from the Wharton School of Business, Steven Covey, PHD, Penn University, who lists of seven habits that every good manager should cultivate:

1. Be Proactive – try to control your environment instead of your environment controlling you.
2. Begin With the End in Mind – This is a strategy developed earlier by a chess champion from Cuba, Capablanca, who ruled chess for twenty years because he analyzed the game from the end rather than from the beginning.
3. Set your priorities to achieve your goal based on #2
4. Think Win-Win
5. Seek first to understand and seek first to be understood
6. Synergize – or creative cooperation to achieve a goal
7. Sharpen the Saw – Learn From Failed Plan A

This should be followed by Seven Bad Habits You Should Never Cultivate as a Manager by Barry Maher, a lifelong consultant for CEOs and Boards in various companies.

1) They rely on other people for their thinking. Whatever the idea of the moment happens to be, that's what they believe. They're not only up on all the latest clichés and buzzwords, they pride themselves on it.

2) No matter how much they may prattle on about openness, inclusiveness, innovative thinking and tolerance, they insist upon conformity. And obedience.

3) Like a cheap politician, they never miss an opportunity to talk about their leadership skills, figuring that if they proclaim that they're leaders frequently enough, someone might actually follow them. True leadership, on the other hand, means never have to tell someone you're a leader.

4) They believe their own BS. Or desperately try to.

5) They'd take credit for the sunrise, if they thought they could get anyone to believe it. They're certain they're responsible for anything their people might accomplish—though failures, mistakes and screw-ups are obviously someone else's fault.

6) They're sure their own successes are the result of their superiority and/or their favor in the eyes of God. Other people are lucky, started with silver spoons hanging out of various orifices, or just butt kissed their way to the top.

7) On the subject of butts, in spite of all their constant claims to the contrary, their actions are guided by the one overriding commandment of their universe: To Thine Own Butt Be True. They cover theirs, whatever the cost. Though the cost is usually borne by someone else.

DEFINE THESE TERMS
1. Exporting 36 – selling your goods to another country
2. Importing36 – buying products from another country
3. Free Trade 37 – no such thing. Movement across borders of goods and services that are not interfered with by other countries or companies.
4. Comparative Advantage Theory -37 – buy what you don't have

from countries that have a lot of it, and sell what you have a lot of to countries that don't have much of it.

5. Absolute Advantage – 38 – monopoly or niche
6. Balance of Trade – 40 – ratio of imports to exports
7. Trade Deficit -40 – occurs when you import more than you export
8. Trade Surplus -40 – occurs when you export more than you import
9. Foreign Direct Investment – 42 – buying property or businesses in foreign nations
10. Licensing 44- -right to manufacture or trademark in another country for a fee
11. Franchising 46- right to use a national company name in a city or town.
12. Contract Manufacturing -46 – goods produced cheaply in another country under a domestic brand (outsourcing)
13. Joint venture -47 – two or more companies combining resources for a project
a. Shared tech
b. Shared marketing (advertising) and management
c. Entry into difficult foreign markets
d. Shared risk
14. Strategic Alliance47 – a long-term partnership between two or more companies in order to get a competitive advantage – UPS and Kinkos
15. Exchange rate52 – one country's currency value in relation to another country's currency value
16. Devaluation 52 – the lowering of the value of your currency
17. Inflation 52 – lower buying power of currency
18. Deflation52- higher buying power of currency
19. Countertrading53 – trading in goods and services rather than currency
20. Trade protectionism55 – assessing taxes on imports to keep prices high for domestic products
21. Tariff55- a tax on imports
22. Import quota55 – an artificial limit on the amount of a product one can import from another country
23. Embargo56 (economic sanctions) – ban on trade with certain countries for various reasons
24. GATT 57-international tariff-lowering agreement

25. WTO 57 – World Trade Organization – organization that mediates trades disputes
26. Common market 58 – a group of countries from a similar region of the world that cooperate economically
27. NAFTA 59– an agreement among US, Canada and Mexico to reduce border restrictions and limits on trade.

FUN ESSAYS! (This is How We Twist the Truth In Advertising!)

HW 2 – In addition to defining the terms answer these questions: one paragraph each

1. Discuss the growing importance of the global market
2. Discuss variables affecting importing and exporting
3. How does a strategic alliance work?
4. What are the advantages and disadvantages of trade protectionism?
5. How had ecommerce affected trade?

Internet Resources for this lesson

General Reference
http://www.askmrmovies.com

Global Markets
www.time.com/time/globalbusiness/

Strategic Alliances
www.smallbusinessnotes.com/

Tafero's Lesson Plan of Day - Introduction to Business 101 - Ethics - Three

Lesson 3 – Ethics

1. Ethics70-societal standards of moral behavior as to what is right and wrong
Example: downloading music and movies; ethical? In US no, in China yes. Depends on the society. That is why there are no movie rental stores in China and thousands of them in the US. Napster challenged the US system and eventually lost (but not before millions, including myself, downloaded tons of free music).

2. Basic Texts for Ethics71
 The Analects, the Bible, the Koran, Aristotle and Shakespeare all apply the Golden Rule: Do unto others as you would have them do unto you.

Take test on page 74

3. Compliance-based ethics codes76- illegal behavior
4. Integrity-based ethics codes76- acting counter to accepted social morals
5. Corporate social responsibility78- concern for society by business- like Bill Gates giving away half of his billions
6. Corporate Philanthropy78-charitable donations to nonprofit groups
7. Corporate responsibility 78- hiring minorities, safe products,protecting the environment, safe workplace and using energy efficiently.
8. Corporate policy 78 – official stance of a company on a political or social issue
9. Insider Trading81 – using inside company information to enrich yourself, family or friends.
10. Social audit84- evaluating a company's social contributions
11. Judiciary92-legal system of a country
12. Business law 93-legal framework of a business
13. Statutory law93-written laws
14. Common law93- unwritten laws

15. Precedent93- how certain legal situations have been decided in the past
16. Administrative agencies93- governmental laws
17. Tort94- wrongful act that causes damage to a person's body, property or reputation
18. Negligence94 – damage caused by unintentional harm or injury
19. Product liability94- product torts
20. Patent96- exclusive right to an invention
21. Copyright97-intellectual property rights
22. Trademark97 – legally protected name, symbol or design

Class Assignment: Analyze American laws passed over the last 100 years or so to protect the American consumer. Does China have laws similar to these? Are they enforced? If they do not, why doesn't China have a law for each of these American laws?

HOMEWORK

HW 3 – In addition to the terms defined above, answer these essay questions: (one paragraph)

1. Why is legality only the beginning of an ethical question?
2. What is management's role in setting ethical standards?
3. What is the difference between compliance based and integrity based ethics codes?
4. How can American businesses influence the ethical behavior of other countries and how can Chinese businesses influence the ethical behavior of other countries? How do they differ?

Internet Resources for this lesson

General Reference

http://www.askmmovies.com

Ethics
www.wisegeek.com/what-is-business-ethics.htm

Chinese Ethics
www.scu.edu/ethics/.../business-china.html

Tafero's Lesson Plan of Day - Introduction to Business 101 - Choosing a Form of Business

Lesson 5 – Choosing a Form of Business Ownership

1. Sole proprietorship110 – a company owned by one person
2. Partnership110 – a company owned by two or more people
3. Corporation110 –a company legally separate from its owners
Advantages of a Sole Proprietorship111
a. Ease of starting and ending the business
b. Being your own boss
c. Pride of ownership
d. Leaving a legacy
e. Retention of company profit
f. No special taxes
Disadvantages of a Sole Proprietorship111
a. Unlimited liability – personal risk
b. Limited financial resources
c. Management difficulties
d. Overwhelming time commitment
e. Few fringe benefits
f. Limited growth
g. Limited life span
Advantages of Partnerships113
a. More financial resources
b. Shared management
c. Longer survival
d. No special taxes
Disadvantages of Partnerships114
a. Unlimited liability
b. Division of profits

c. Disagreement
d. Difficulty of termination
Advantages of Corporations117
a. Limited liability
b. More investment money
c. Size
d. Perpetual life
e. Ease of ownership change
f. Ease of gathering talented employees
g. Separation of ownership from management
Disadvantages of Corporations119
a. Extensive paperwork
b. Double taxation
c. Two tax returns
d. Size
e. Difficulty of termination
f. Conflict among stockholders and board of trustees
g. Initial cost

4. Merger124- two firms forming one company
5. Acquisitions124 – buying another company

Advantages of a Franchise
a. Management and marketing assistance
b. Personal ownership
c. Nationally recognized name
d. Financial advice and assistance
e. Lower failure rate (14%)

Disadvantages of a Franchise
a. Large start-up costs
b. Shared profit
c. Management regulation
d. Coattail effect – (other franchise problems might affect yours)
e. Fraudulent franchises
6. Cooperative133- a socialist form of early Chinese farm communes.

If You're Good, I'll Give You Some Essays! (If you're bad, I'll Give you Extra Essays)

HW 4 – In addition to the half dozen terms in Chapter 4, answer the following essay questions in ESSAY form. (one paragraph)

1. Study chart on page 123 and choose one model in an essay question for homework. In your response, state why you have chosen one of these models.
2. Compare the advantages and disadvantages of a proprietorship.
3. Compare the advantages and disadvantages of a partnership
4. Compare the advantages and disadvantages of a corporation
5. Compare the advantages and disadvantages of a franchise

Internet Resources for this lesson

General Reference

http://www.askmrmovies.com

Advantages of Corporations
www.e-law.bc.ca/art_corpstructure.html

Advantages of Franchises

www.businesslink.gov.uk

Tafero's Lesson Plan of Day - Introduction to Business 101 - Management Leadership - Six

Chapter 5 – Management, Leadership and Employee Empowerment

1. Management143- process used to accomplish organizational goals through planning, leading and control.
2. Planning143-anticipating trends and determining the best strategies and tactics to achieve your objective
3. Organizing143-designing the structure of the organization and creating conditions and systems to achieve goals and objectives.
4. Leading144-creating a vision by guiding, training, coaching and motivating others to work effectively to achieve the organization'sgoals and objectives.
5. Controlling144- establishing clear standards
6. Vision145- purpose and values in addition to goals and objectives
a. Organizational self-concept
b. Company Philosophy and goals
c. Long-term survival
d. Customer Needs
e. Social Responsibility
f. Nature of the Company's product or service
7. Goals145 – Broad long-term accomplishments
8. Objectives145 – Specific short-term plans to move positively toward the organization's goals.
9. SWOT146 analysis – strengths, weaknesses, opportunities and threats (see 5.3)
10. Strategic Planning146-determines the major goals of the organization. Primary strategic planning for the vast majority of major companies in the world generally include the following: Stock market price, market share, and sales (which usually means selecting the best advertising campaign)
11. Tactical Planning147 – is the process of developing detailed, short-term statements about what is to be done, who is to do it, how and where it will be done.
12. Operational Planning148-is the process of setting work standards and schedules necessary to implement the company's tactical objectives.
13. Contingency Planning148*****-extremely important element of strategic management. PLAN A NEVER WORKS! So you must always have a plan B,C,D and so on. Why doesn't plan A

work? Because no one can predict the future, so elements of planning must ALWAYS be adjusted for unforeseen developments AND the process is CONTINUOUS. No plan is useful unless the process is continuous and cyclical.

14. Decision-Making148 – is choosing among two or more alternatives.
a. Define the situation
b. Describe and collect needed data (R&D)
c. Develop Alternatives
d. Develop Agreement among those involved (consensus)
e. Decide which alternative is best
f. Do what is indicated (implementation)
g. Determine whether the course of action is a good one to follow up with Plan B

EXAMPLES OF DECISION- MAKING***** Save money by not having a child? Or have a child and be much poorer and have much less time? Having a child means you will have to work longer and harder. Do you want to do that? Would you choose a good paying job over a child? Over living with your family? Over living with your husband or wife? Would you be willing to relocate for a high-paying job that would mean giving up a currently successful relationship?

15. Problem Solving149 – process of solving every-day problems
16. Brainstorming149- coming up with numerous ideas at one time and weighing the alternatives
17. Organization chart149-visual device that shows relationships among people within an organization and that divides the work among them.
18. Top Management149- CEO and Board of Trustees over 90% of the time.
19. Middle Management150-managers, department heads and other higher management
20. Supervisory Management150- those who directly manage entry level and beginning workers
21. Technical Skills151-ability to perform tasks in a specific discipline
22. Human Relation Skills151-communication and motivational skills
23. Conceptual Skills151-vision skills include seeing the big picture.

24. Staffing153-recruiting and hiring the best available people
25. Managing Diversity154 – providing tokens to keep government officials off your ass or to fool the public (as in Chinese schools that try to teach English with nine Chinese teachers and one native English teacher) OR actually building a system and climate that unites different people in a common pursuit as in a team.
26. Autocratic Leadership156 – trying to do it all yourself; a very bad strategy, generally speaking. Good for quick decisions, however.
27. Democratic Leadership156 –everyone in the company participates in discussion of issues. Good in theory, but time-consuming in actual practice. Many decisions must be made quickly and this process is not conducive to speed. When time is not a factor, a very good process.
28. Free-Rein Leadership157 – Managers set objectives and allow employees to reach the goals by whatever means they prefer to use. This is a common approach in the sales industry. You meet my sales quota and I don't care if you are a manly man wearing a frilly dress while singing opera in the middle of the street. Also called Bottom-Line management in the US. (give example in accounting)
29. Enabling159-giving workers the tools they need to succeed.
30. Knowledge (Data) Management 160- communicating ALL the R&D your company has in its database to all the appropriate people and departments AT THE SAME TIME.

HW 5 – In addition to defining the above terms, answer the following essay questions:

1. How does the current business environment affect management function?
2. Describe the four functions of management.
3. Relate the planning process and decision making to the accomplishment of company goals.
4. Describe the organizing function of management.
5. Describe the various leadership styles.
6. Summarize the five steps of the control function of management.

Internet Resources for this lesson

General Reference

http://www.askmrmovies.com

Functions of Management

www.managementstudyguide.com/management_functions.htm

Leadership Styles

www.nwlink.com/~donclark/leader/leadstl.html

Tafero's Lesson Plan of Day - Introduction to Business 101 - Adapting to New Models - Seven

Lesson 6 – Adapting Organizations to Today's Markets

1. Economies of Scale171 – Reduction of Production costs whenraw materials are purchased in bulk
2. Fayol's Theories171
a. Unity of Command – having only ONE boss.
b. Hierarchy of Authority – ladder
c. Division of Labor – a questionable process of strictly dividing functions
d. Team first – team or group comes before the individual
e. Authority – someone must always be in charge
f. Centralization – another form of authority
g. Communication – essential for efficiency
h. Order – messy workplaces lead to messy results
3. Weber's Theories173- similar to Fayol but also include:
a. Job descriptions – so you know what your responsibilities are

b. Written rules

c. Records

d. Consistent procedures

e. Staffing and Promotion Based on qualifications and Performance (Confucianism)

4. Bureaucracy173-An organization with many layers of managers; each with their own set of rules

5. Centralized Authority175-top-down decision-making

6. Decentralized Authority175-bottom up decision-making

Advantages of Centralized Authority (China model)-175

a. Greater top management control

b. More efficiency

c. Simpler distribution system

d. Stronger image

Disadvantages of Centralized Authority175

a. Less responsive to local needs

b. Less empowerment

c. Interorganizational conflict

d. Lower morale away from central government (Beijing)

Advantages of Decentralized Authority (US model)175

a. More responsive to local needs

b. More empowerment of local workers

c. Local decision-making

d. Higher morale in local areas

Disadvantages of Decentralized Authority175

a. Less efficient

b. Complex Distribution

c. Less top-management control

d. Weaker national image

7. Span of Control176 – optimum number of subordinates a boss should have.

Variables for Span of Control Include:

a. Capability of the manager

b. Capability of the subordinates

c. Geographic proximity

d. Functional Similarity

e. Coordination Difficulty

f. Planning Demands

g. Function Complexity

8. Tall Organization Structure177- a highly bureaucratic company with many layers
9. Flat Organization Structure177-a company with few layers of control.

Advantages of Tall Structure178
a. More control by top management
b. More chances for advancement
c. Greater specialization
d. Closer Supervision

Disadvantages of Tall Structure178
a. Less empowerment
b. Higher costs
c. Delayed decision-making
d. Less responsive to customers (citizens)

Advantages of Flat Structure178
a. Reduced costs
b. More responsive to customers (citizens)
c. Faster decision-making
d. More empowerment

Disadvantages of Flat Structure178
a. Fewer chances of advancement
b. Overworked managers
c. Loss of control
d. Less management expertise

10. Departmentalization 178- dividing of organizational functions into separate units.

Advantages of Departmentalization178
a. Employees develop skill in depth
b. Company can centralize resources and experts for that area
c. Good coordination

Disadvantages of Departmentalization178
a. Lack of communication between departments
b. Individuals within a department will consider its goals ahead of the company's goals
c. Company response will be slower
d. Company training becomes narrower

Organization Models181
a. Line organizations
b. Line and staff organizations
c. Matrix-style organizations
d. Cross-functional self-managed teams (sales)

11. Line Organizations 181-top to bottom
12. Line and Staff Organization181 – chain of command (line) and staff (advise and assist chain)
13. Matrix-Style Organization182-specialists who work together (as in advertising teams)
14. Cross-Functional Self-Managed Teams184 – where everyone does everything (not always the best solution)
15. Networking (Guanxi)185 – linking organizations or people for common goals
16. Real Time185 – the time it takes for something to actually happen
17. Transparency185 – openness
18. Benchmarking186-comparing your results with the highest attainable
19. Outsourcing187 – assigning jobs outside your organization to save money
20. Core Competancies187 – products or services your company can provide better than anyone else (also known as niches)
21. Restructuring187-reorganizing an organization to save money or to be more efficient (usually the former)
22. Inverted Organization188 – where the boss comes last and the workers first; if anyone has ever seen any example of this in China (or any other country), please let me know.
23. Reengineering188-radical redesign and/or improvement. IBM a good example because they are highly incompetent and need it badly. Lost their market in computers to Lenovo.
24. Organizational Culture189-widely shared values within an organization
25. Formal Organization190-highly structured and bureaucratic
26. Informal Organization190-loosely organized and relatively flat in structure.

Get Organized! Here is the CEO of EasternStudiesDatabase.cn – Be Like Him!

HW 6 – In addition to the above definitions answer the following essay questions:

1. Discuss Fayol and Weber
2. Discuss issues involved in structuring organizations
3. Describe and differentiate the various organizational models
4. Discuss how restructuring, organizational culture and informal organizations can help businesses change.

Internet Resources for this lesson

General Reference

http://www.askmrmovies.com

Weber

www.bustingbureaucracy.com/excerpts/weber.htm

Organizational Models

www.slideshare.net

Tafero's Lesson Plan of Day - Introduction to Business 101 - Marketing - Eight

Lesson 8 – Marketing (Selling-Advertising) – Building Customer and Stakeholder Relationships

1. Marketing 234 – process of planning and executing the conception, pricing, promotion and distribution of goods.

2. Marketing Concept235 – includes:

A. customer orientation – finding out what customers want and provide it for them .

B. Service orientation – make sure everyone in the organization has the same objective-customer satisfaction

C. A profit orientation – focus on those goods and services that will earn the most profit and enable the organization to survive and expand to serve more consumer wants and needs.

3. Consumer relationship management 235 – process of learning as much as possible about customers and doing everything you can to satisfy them.

4. The Marketing Mix236 – product, price, place and promotion

5. Product238- any physical good, service or idea that satisfies a want or need of consumers

6. Test Marketing239-testing products among potential users

7. Brand name239 - a word, letter, groups of words or letters or logos that differentiates one seller's goods from another

8. Promotion 240- techniques sellers use to inform people and motivate them to buy their products or services

9. Marketing Research (R&D)-241 – analysis of markets to determine opportunities and challenges and to find the information needed to make good decisions

10. The Marketing Research Process242*****-

a. Define the question, problem or opportunity and determine the current status

b. Collect data for the current status

c. Analyze the data

d. Choose the best solution to go forward in the process and implement it

11. Secondary data242-using someone else's research

12. Primary data242- doing your own research

13. Focus group243 – small group of people who meet to discuss and communicate their opinions

14. Environmental Scanning244- examining global, tech, social competitive and economic variables

15. Consumer Market247- consists of all the individuals or households that want goods and services and have the resources to buy them

16. B2B Market247-consists of all the individuals and organizations that want goods and services to use in producing

other goods and services to sell, rent or supply goods to others.

17. Market Segmentation247- process of dividing the total market into several groups whose members have similar characteristics.

18. Target Marketing247-selection which groups (market segments) an organization can serve profitably.

19. Geographic segmentation248- dividing the market by geography (location)

20. Demographic Segmentation248 – dividing the market by age, income, and education.

21. Psychographic Segmentation248- dividing the market by values, interests and attitudes

22. Benefit Segmentation248- dividing the market by which benefits are preferred by the customer

23. Usage Segmentation248- dividing the market by the volume consumed by each segment of the market.

24. Niche marketing248-finding a small, but profitable market segment and designing products for them.

25. One-to-One Marketing 249 – developing unique goods and services one customer at a time.

26. Mass marketing249 – developing products and promotions to please large groups of people

27. Relationship marketing250- moving away from mass production and moving toward custom-made goods and services for current customers.

28. The Consumer Decision-Making Process253- *****

a. learning - can be from experience or from information

b. reference group – schoolboy, college student, entry level worker, manager

c. culture – set of values, attitudes and ways of doing things for each of the reference groups

d. subculture – set of values, attitudes and ways of doing things for a particular group within the reference group.

e. Reinforcement – reinforcing the decision of the customer that has bought your product with reassuring data.

29. Stakeholder marketing257 – maintaining mutually beneficial exchange relationships over time with all the stakeholders of an organization

30. Green Product257- environmentally sound product

Essays
1. Discuss profit and non-profit marketing
2. Discuss the four Ps of the Marketing Mix
3. Describe the Marketing Research Process
4. Discuss Marketing segmentation
5. How does B2B differ from consumer marketing?
6. Discuss stakeholder marketing and customer relationship management

Internet Resources for this lesson

General Reference

http://www.askmrmovies.com

Marketing Theory

www.businessperformancemaximized.com/.../marketing_theory_and_business_r...

Segmentation

www.thetimes100.co.uk/theory/theory--segmentation--246.php

Tafero's Lesson Plan of Day - Introduction to Business 101 - Pricing - Nine

Lesson 9 – Developing Pricing Products and Services

1. Value266-good quality at a fair price
2. Total product offer267-quality, price and service+
3. Product line 268- group of similar products intended for a

similar market

4. Product mix268- combination of all product lines with different product lines

5. Product differentiation270 – the creation of real or perceived differences in products

6. Convenience goods and services270- products consumers want frequently with a minimum of effort

7. Shopping goods and services 270- products comparing value, quality, price and style

8. Specialty goods and services270-products with unique characteristics and brands

9. Unsought goods and services 271 – products consumers seldom think about

10. Industrial Goods271 – B2B goods purchased to produce other products

11. Brand274-name,symbol or design that identifies goods or services and distinguishes it from the competition

12. Brand name -274 – part of the brand that identifies goods and services

13. Trademark-274- a brand that has exclusive legal protection.

14. Manufacturer brand name 274 – brand names of companies that distribute nationally

15. Dealer brands 274 – brands that carry the local retailers name instead of the national name

16. Generic goods 275 – non-branded products that sell for much less than brand names

17. Knockoff brands 275 – Chinese and other countries' goods that imitate real quality brands at low prices

18. Brand equity275-awareness, quality. Loyalty, images and emotions associated with the brand

19. Brand loyalty275- degree of customer satisfaction

20. Brand awareness275- how quickly a brand comes to mind when mentioned

21. Brand association276- linking a brand to other favorable images

22. Brand manager 276- has direct responsibility for one brand or product line.

23. New Product Development Process******-277- 1. Idea, 2 product screening 3. Product analysis 4. Development, 5. Commercialization (bring to market)

24. Product screening 277- process used to reduce the number of new product ideas
25. Product analysis277- make cost and sales estimates
26. Concept testing 278-testing your product on consumers
27. Commercialization278- promotion, advertising and sales campaigns
28. Product life cycle-279 – what happens to sales and profits over time*****introduction, growth, maturity and decline
29. Target costing284- satisfying customers and profit margins at the same time
30. Competition based pricing 284 – Chinese model – basing your prices on the competition
31. Price leadership284- setting the price for a good or service in the market
32. Break-even analysis285 – the least you can do to break even
33. Total fixed costs285- expenses that seldom change
34. Variable costs285- expenses that vary from month to month
35. Skimming price strategy286 – overpricing the item while it is new or scarce
36. Penetration strategy286- pricing a product low to get high initial sales
37. Everyday low pricing286 – Walmart and Home Depot strategies; no sales
38. High-low pricing strategy286- original high prices and then a big sale to reduce them
39. Bundling286- pricing two products together as a unit
40. Psychological pricing286 – 1.99 instead of 2.00
41. Non-price strategies 288 – added value, education of consumers and establishing relationships
42. Added value 288- free home delivery
43. Educating consumers288 – home depot teachers customers how to fix homes
44. Establish relationships288-customers pay for more to people they know

Essay questions for Lesson 9 in addition to the above definitions:

1. Discuss a total product offer
2. List the functions of packaging
3. Discuss brands, brand names and trademarks
4. Discuss the product life cycle
5. Discuss various pricing objectives and strategies
6. Discuss non-pricing strategies

Internet Resources for this lesson

General Reference

http://www.askmrmovies.com

Branding

www.klminc.com/branding/theoryofbrand.htm

Pricing Theory

www.daviddfriedman.com/.../Price_Theory/.../PThy_Chapter_11.html

Tafero's Lesson Plan of Day - Introduction to Business 101 - Financial Information - Ten

Chapter 10 – Understanding Financial Information and Accounting

1. Accounting298-recording of financial transactions for information inside the company

2. CMA -299- Certified Management Accountant- someone professionally trained within a company to do accounting. Rigid testing is required to become a CMA

3. Financial accounting -300-information for people outside the company

4. Annual report 300- accounting on a yearly basis

5. Private accountants 300- accountants that work for a private company

6. Public accountants300- accountants who will work for anyone

7. Certified Public Accountants – accountants just like CMAs, but not working for any single company

8. GAAP- 300- Generally Accepted Accounting Principles – Methods that were ignored and caused the Global Financial Crisis are now currently being "rediscovered".

9. Auditing -301 – Internal Accounting investigators

10. Independent audit – 301 – Outside accounting investigators

11. Tax Accountant – 302 – an accountant specially trained in taxation

12. Government and Non-Profit Accounting 302- accountants trained for non-profits or zero-based budgeting.

13. Bookkeeping (ledgers) 303 – number entries of debits and credits

14. Journal303- the documentation of the entries of debits and credits

15. Double-Entry bookkeeping303- two entries in the journal and the ledgers . Example: you spend 100Y on supplies. You credit cash 100Y and you debit supplies 100Y. It tells you where the money is going*****(this system was abandoned during the global financial crisis; a number of CREATIVE accounting methods were practiced instead that showed highly inflated profits and eventually, destroyed most companies who did not practice GAAP).

16. The Accounting Cycle 303-*****-a. Analyze bill or payment, b. record transaction in journal, c. transfer journal entries to the ledger, d. take a trial balance, e. prepare a financial statement based on these numbers, f. analyze the financial statement (repeat the process each quarter)

17. Assets=Liabilities+Owner's Equity – Fundamental Accounting Equation 306 (another way of stating this equations is Assets-Liabilities = net profit (owner's equity)306

18. Balance sheet 306-financial statement of a company's profit or loss at a specific point in time
19. Assets306 –economic resources with a cash value306
20. Liquidity 308 – how fast you can turn your assets into cash
21. Assets=Current Assets (cash), fixed assets (desks and chairs), intangible assets patents, copyrights, goodwill (guanxi). Of these, only Current Assets and Fixed Assets (in wholesale form) can be used to determine liquidity
22. Liabilities308 – Money you owe
23. Owners Equity309 – What is left over in assets after you pay the money you owe
24. Retained earnings 309 – money kept in the business and not taken out in profits
25. Income Statement 310 – same as 17.
26. Revenue310 – value of what is received for goods sold (cash and goods or services)
27. Cost of Goods Sold311 – wholesale cost of what you sell for one item or all items*****EXTREMELY IMPORTANT (cost accounting is considered to be one of the most important of ALL accounting procedures)
28. Operating Expenses312 – rent, salaries of help, office bills, transportation
29. Cash Flow Statement312 – includes operations (cash transactions), investments (cash being used in securities or real estate), and financing (cost of a loan)
30. Cash flow314- assets vs liabilities in cash
31. Depreciation315 – the systematic write-off of property or goods
32. FIFO316 – Inventory sold as first in, first out
33. LIFO316-Inventory sold as last in, first out; not good for persishibles, but ok for non-foods.
34. Ratio analysis317-breaking down the big numbers and forming simple fractions and percentages from them.

HW for Lesson 10 in addition to the definitions above answer these essays:

1. Why is financial information and accounting important?
2. Discuss the different types of accounting
3. What is the difference between bookkeeping and accounting? Mention the accounting cylcle
4. Discuss Depreciation, LIFO and FIFO
5. Discuss ratio analysis

Internet Resources for this lesson

General Reference

http://www.askmrmovies.com

The Accounting Cycle

www.transtutors.com/.../accounting/accounting.../accounting-theory/accou...

Ratio Analysis

www.thetimes100.co.uk/theory/theory--ratio-analysis--301.php

Tafero's Lesson Plan of Day - Introduction to Business 101 - Financial Management - Eleven

Lesson 11 – Financial Management

1. Finance332-is a function of the business that acquires funds for the company
2. Financial management332- managing the companies resources to meet goals
3. Financial managers332-examine data and make recommendations for improvement
4. Short-term forecast334-one year or less guessing

5. Cash-flow forecast334-monthly or quarterly cash plans and guessing
6. Long-term forecast335-5-10 year guessing
7. Budget335- guessing revenues and expenditures for fixed periods of time
8. Capital budget-336-spending plans
9. Cash budget336- revenue and spending plans
10. Financial control337-comparing reality with your plans and making adjustments
11. Capital expenditures341- major investments in the budget
12. Short-term financing341-one year loan
13. Long-term financing341-loans for longer than one year
14. Debt-financing341-loans other than normal bank loans
15. Trade credit343-buy goods and services now and pay later
16. Promissory note343-contract to repay loan
17. Secured loan345-loan made with collateral
18. Unsecured loan345- loan made without collateral
19. Revolving credit agreement345 – frequent loans
20. Commercial paper346-unsecured promissory notes
21. Term-loan agreement348-promissory note in installments
22. Risk/return trade-off348- the greater the risk, the higher the interest rate
23. Indentured bonds349-company or government loan
24. Secured bonds349-company or government loans with collateral (rare for countries)
25. Unsecured bonds349- usually government loans, with occasional famous companies
26. Venture capital350-investing in new business with high upside
27. Leverage352- using collateral to get more capital
28. Cost of capital352 – all loans cost X amount of money

In addition to these definitions answer the following essays

1. Why is finance important to a company?
2. Outline the financial planning process
3. Why do companies need operating funds and how can they get them?
4. Discuss short-term financing
5. Discuss long-term financing

Internet Resources for this lesson

General Reference

http://www.askmrmovies.com

Finance Theory

www.ltnielsen.com/

Financial Planning
www.financial-planning.com

Tafero's Lesson Plan of the Day - Intro to Business 101 - Securities Markets - Twelve

Lesson 12 – Securities Markets: Financing and Investing Opportunities

1. IPO -360- first public offering of a company's stock
2. Institutional Investors361 – Banks
3. Bond361 – corporate loan
4. Interest362-additional payment given on a loan
5. -Maturity Date362-date payment of interest is due on loan
6. Debenture Bond363-non-collateral bonds
7. Sinking fund364-money put aside to pay bonds
8. Stocks365-shares of ownership in a company

9. Stock Certificate365-evidence of stock ownership
10. Dividends365-distributed profits of a company in addition to stock value.
11. Preferred stock366 – stock with dividends and first liquidation rights
12. Common stock367-stock liquidated after preferred stock
13. Stock exchange367-an organization whose members buy and sell stocks
14. OTC368- over the counter stocks not listed on the main exchange
15. NASDAQ368- a stock exchange dealing with lesser-valued stocks
16. SEC369- a government regulatory commission for stocks, investors and brokers
17. Prospectus369-a brochure describing the investment stock
18. Investment risk374-less risk; less reward
19. Yield374-expected rate of return vs actual rate of return
20. Duration374- length of time your money is committed
21. Liquidity374- how quickly you can convert to cash
22. Tax Consequences374- how much you must pay on capital gains
23. Capital gains376- the profit you make on stock investments
24. Stock splits376- 100 a share stocks become two at 50
25. Mutual funds377-investment in a group of stocks and bonds at the same time
26. Diversification378-investing in several different alternative markets
27. Junk bonds379-risky bonds with no collateral
28. Buying stock on margin379-dangerous method of investing as little as 50% while getting 100% ownership of stock.
29. Commodity exchange 379-buying and selling of precious metals
30. Futures markets380-buying goods in the future at present prices
31. Dow Jones Industrial Average383-average cost of 30 industrial stocks for one day
32. Program trading385- computerized buying and selling

Answer these essay questions in addition to the definitions above:

1. What are the functions of securities markets and the role of investment bankers?
2. Discuss the advantages and disadvantages of bonds
3. Discuss the advantages and disadvantages of stocks
4. Discuss stock exchanges
5. Discuss mutual funds.
6. Discuss high-risk investments

Internet Resources for this lesson

General Reference

http://www.askmrmovies.com

Securities Markets
www.ifc.org/ifcext/gfm.nsf/.../SM-Brochure1/.../SM-Brochure1.pdf

High-Risk Investments
www.askmen.com/money/investing_150/178_investing.html

Tafero's Lesson Plan of the Day - Intro to Business 101 - Understanding Money - Thirteen

Lesson 13 – Understanding Money and Financial Institutions

1. Money 394- anything people accept as payment for goods and services
2. Barter394-trading goods and services
3. Portability394- the ability to carry your assets
4. Divisibility394-different values for coins
5. Stability394-value of your currency
6. Durability394-coins last a long time
7. Uniqueness395- hard to counterfeit coins
8. Money supply396-amount of money a government prints
9. Reserve requirement-398-percentage of money that must be available in banks
10. Open-market operations399-buying and selling of government bonds
11. Commercial bank402- profit-seeking organization that takes deposits from individuals and companies
12. Time Deposit403- a savings account
13. CD403- Certificate of Deposit is a time sensitive savings account
14. Savings and Loan 404- banks that specialize in savings and mortgages
15. Credit Unions405- non-profit cooperatives that provide services for various unions
16. Pension funds406-money put aside for retirement by companies
17. FDIC- 407an agency that insure the savings of citizens in the US
18. EFT-410 Electronic Funds Transfer allows online transactions
19. Debit card-410- electronic checking account
20. Smart card410 – credit card, debit card, phone card and driverslicense and more
21. Letter of credit411- promise of a bank to pay an amount of money
22. Banker's acceptance411- promise to pay a specific amount at a specific time
23. World Bank412- Finances economic development in developing countries
24. IMF412- International Monetary Fund- moderates currencies in world markets

In addition to the above definitions, please answer these essay questions

1. Discuss money and how its value is determined
2. Discuss the various institutions of the US banking system
3. Discuss the FDIC
4. Discuss the future of banking
5. Discuss International Banking

Since you all got the cash money guess wrong, you all have to do the ESSAYS.

Internet Resources for this lesson

General Reference

http://www.askmrmovies.com

Value of Money
www.westegg.com/inflation/

Institutional Banking
www.bnz.co.nz/institutional-banking

Part Two of Business for Beginners - Marketing

Marketing Management

Arthur H Tafero

Tafero's Lesson Plan of Day - Marketing Management - The Marketing Environment - One

Lesson 1 - The Marketing Environment

a. How grade is calculated – Grades are calculated on five basic elements: In-Class Activities (ICAs) = 20%, Simulation One – Non-Profit Ad = 20%, Simulation Two For-Profit Ad = 20%, Final Presentation of Company with Paper = 20%, Final Exam = 20%
b. Company designations for papers – Each student will be assigned a major Fortune 500 company (or in China, a major Chinese company) for Final Presentation purposes
c. Team designations for simulations – Each member of the class will be assigned to a team on the first day of class. These teams will be responsible for Simulations One and Two. Simulations will consist of music, photos, English text, Chinese text (if course in China), and appropriate content for ad: not to exceed two minutes
d. Presentations – Each student will present their designated company in a PPT presentation as well as in a three-page paper highlighting a current Market Share, Sales for one year and Stock Market price fluctuations for one year.
e. Homework ICA – ICA will either be completed in class or handed in before the beginning of the next class
f. Examples of successful simulations – Well-made ads will be shown on the first day for both the non-profit and profit sector.
g. Final Exams – Final exams will be critical essay questions which address why and how the important elements of the course are used. There will be four questions assigned on Exam day from a pool of eight possible questions.

1. Discuss the differences between marketplaces and marketspaces - pg 9

Marketplace is physical as in Walmart

Marketspace is digital as in the internet like Amazon.com

2. Describe the relationships among the marketing environment, the organizational vision (strategic plan) and the strategic marketing plan.****pgs 9,11,15 and 90

(A) The Marketing Environment (15) consists of the Task Environment (15) which includes the immediate actors involved in producing, distributing and promoting the product and the Broad Environment (15) which consists of these primary components. The main actors of the Task Environment are: the company, suppliers, distributors, dealers, and the target customers. The primary components of the Broad Environment include: the demographic environment, the economic environment, the natural environment, the technological environment, the political-legal environment and the social-cultural environment. These variables must be calculatedwhen formulating the Strategic Plan (90) and the Strategic Marketing Plan (90).

(B) The Strategic Plan or Organizational Vision has three main components: it calls for the management of the company's businesses as an investment portfolio, the assessment of each of these business's strengths by considering the market's growth rate and the company's position in that market, and this Research and Development (R&D), combined with theMarketing Environment, leads to the establishment of a Strategic Marketing Plan.

(C) The Strategic Marketing Plan lays out the target markets (Segmentation (9) and Value Proposition (set of customer benefits) (11) based on opportunities researched by R&D. The information gathered from the Marketing and Task Environments are then combined with the proposed goals of the Strategic and Strategic Marketing Plans

3. Name and define the differences between needs, wants and demands - pg 11

Needs – Basic Human Requirements – air, food, shelter, and clothing – (Maslow)

Additional Needs – education, recreation, entertainment, interpersonal interaction, self-actualization (Maslow)

Wants – Specific items that satisfy our needs. All Americans need food and many of them satisfy that need with a potato. All Asians need food and satisfy that need with rice.

Demands – Are wants for specific products backed by an ability to pay for them. We want a Mercedes Benz, but we only afford a Toyota.

Marketers do not create needs. They influence wants and demands.

4. Discuss relationships and networks in both Chinese (guanxi) and Western terms ****– pg 13

Eastern Relationships are generally created through guanxi (family and friend networking). Strangers to family and friends are generally not included in the circle of business. Nepotism is a negative aspect of strict guanxi. Western Relationships are similar to Eastern Relationships, but are not especially restricted to family and friends. Westerners will do business based strictly on profit motives. (holistic networking or marketing network). Lack of loyalty and distended families are weaknesses of the Western method. Westerners do not care about saving face as much as Easterners.

5. How does the Ebay strategy differ from the Product Concept principle? – pg 17

Basically, the Product Concept states that quality and performance are more valuable to the consumer than low price. This is obviously not a foolproof idea since most people choose McDonalds over better hamburgers at better restaurants. More people buy from Walmart than specialty stores. People may WANT the best television, and there will be some DEMAND for better televisions, but most people are restricted by their personal budgets and most will buy only the best television they can AFFORD to satisfy that NEED. In relationship to Ebay, one can get a much better price for QUALITY goods in private auction houses than one can get on the frugal Ebay buyers listings.

6. Discuss Customer Needs – pg 21

A. Stated Needs – (The customer wants an inexpensive car)
B. Real Needs – (Customer wants a car whose operating cost, not initial price, is low)
C. Unstated Needs – (The Customer expects good service from the dealer)
D. Delight Needs – (The Customer would like the dealer to include a gift with the deal)
E. Secret Needs – (The Customer would like to be seen by his family and/or friends as a savvy consumer.

7. Discuss some variables negatively impacting on Profitability – pg 24

A. Sales Decline – Declining Sales may or may not be remedied
B. Slow Growth – Requires the search for new markets
C. Changing Buying Patterns – Trends change
D. Increasing Competition – Competition decreases profit. More competition decreases your piece of the pie
E. Increasing Marketing Expenditures – advertising (energy use?) and other expenditures will decrease profits.

8. How does the Societal Marketing concept relate to Chinese marketing? Pg 25
Societal Marketing is simply providing customers with additional benefit via a perceived or realcontribution to society. This is closely related to trend recognition because societies tend to have trends that are perceived to be good for society. Examples might include environmentally sound energy usage (conservation), lower fat foods (better health for consumers), and even building good character by wearing sneakers in sports (build character by "Just Doing It" (Nike).
Chinese Societal Marketing is still an open issue. Some think that environmentally sound products will go over well with the mass market in China because of its environmental problems, others think that quality strategies may be the way to go because of the

economic boom within the country. Price-driven strategies seem to always be in place whether the economy is good or bad.

ICA Homework – Essays – Lesson One

Old-Fashioned Marketing

Write One Paragraph on each question.

1. How are marketplaces and marketspaces different?
2. How do the marketing environment, the strategic plan, and the strategic marketing plan all differ?
3. How do needs, wants, and demands differ?
4. How does Eastern networking differ from Western networking?
5. How do customer needs differ?
6. How do some variables affect profitability?

Internet Resources for this lesson:

General Reference Material For All Content

http://www.askmrmovies.com

Strategic Plans

http://www.managementhelp.org/plan_dec/str_plan/str_plan.htm

Profitability

www.investopedia.com

Tafero's Lesson Plan of Day - Marketing Management - Value - Two

Lesson 2 – Value and Organizational Diagnosis

Managerial Marketing

1. Discuss the concepts of Customer Value**** Pg 35
A. Price – Sometimes it is merely price and other times it is total customer cost (evaluation, obtaining, using and disposing the product or service)
B. Quality – consumers often appreciate the benefit of quality over a long period of time or greater effectiveness in a short period of time
C. Benefits – Sometimes the consumer is delighted by the performance or effectiveness of a product that is not normally advertised (an example would be impressing a date with your Mercedes Benz). A more common example would be a secondaryuse of a product (an example would be a container that keeps food from spoiling in an emergency as well as keeping it cold)
D. Convenience – people tend to buy items close to where they live whenever possible or do not wish to spend much time shopping for a product
E. Service – some consumers put great stock in the service of company and will continue to be loyal to that company for many years in the future

2. Discuss the concepts of Customer Satisfaction.
Satisfaction = The difference between what you want and what you get pg 36
A. Strategies include consumer complaint and suggestion systems pg 38
B. Another strategy is the satisfaction survey pg 38
C. The strategy of unannounced inspection (mystery shoppers) is a current trend in marketing pg 38
D. Lost customer analysis conducts an exit survey to try and fix

the problem. Customer Rate Loss is the magic number here and needs to go down or the company will have growing problems. Pg 38

3. Discuss the marketing strategy of MySimon.com – pg 36
MySimon.com uses a data-driven mediation strategy that is unbiased in its analysis. This provides the user with untainted data to make decisions.

4. Define the following as it relates to Marketing: Pg 40

Stakeholders – strategies must satisfy key shareholders
Processes – must be improved over a fixed period of time
Resources – must be allocated in pie fashion throughout the organization

5. Discuss the strategy for PlasticsNet.com marketing – Pg 43

PlasticsNet.com targets businesses who need to do business with other businesses (B2B). This data-driven company then derives a niche from their unbiased information.

6. Discuss the emergence of Web MD – pg 45
WebMD targets individuals who seek medical opinions without actually having to go to a doctor. The site does not recommend procedures like a doctor would, but it does give a massive amount of information about any disease or discomfort you may be having. The user then uses that information to decide whether or not to actually see a physician, or whether they can take care of the problem with less drastic measures. WebMD now has a strong niche in the medical services sector.

7. Discuss the concept of Organizational Diagnosis**** – (not in book) (Columbia U)
(The instructor will use a large diagram of the human body as an example of a company's components).
A. The brain would be represented by the CEO and Board of Trustees utilizing research gathered by trusted professional researchers.
B. The heart and blood would represented by cash (as in cash

flow)

C. The legs would be represented by the sales force

D. The stomach would be represented by the company's competiveness and resistance to competition

E. Other body parts could also be made analogous (do not use the bladder or kidneys as wasting money unless absolutely necessary)

If there is something wrong with one part of the body, it adversely affects the whole body and needs to be fixed as soon as possible.

8. Discuss the Brick and Click strategies of the following – pg 47

A Gibson Guitars

B Liberty Mutual

C Avon

D JC Penny

9. Discuss the dos and don'ts of Social Actions affecting Buyer-Seller relationships: pg 54

A. Initiate positive calls; don't wait for callbacks

B. Recommend; don't justify

C. Use phone; not correspondence

D. Show appreciation; don't take the consumer for granted

E. Make service suggestions; don't wait for requests

F. Use "we " language; don't use "you and the company product"

G. Prevent problems from occurring; don't wait for them to occur

H. Keep it simple; don't be complex

I. Speak of the Future; not of the Past

J. Accept responsibility; don't pass on the blame

ICA Homework – Essays – Lesson Two

Dating Value for Veronica

Write One Paragraph on each question

1. Why is customer value important to your business?
2. Why is customer satisfaction important?
3. How would you perform an organizational diagnosis?
4. How do social actions affect buyer-seller relationships?

Internet Resources for this lesson:

General Reference Material For All Content

http://www.askmrmovies.com

Customer Value
www.businessdictionary.com/definition/customer-value.html

Organizational Diagnosis
www.rapidbi.com/management/organizationaldiagnosisanddevelopment

Tafero's Lesson Plan of Day - Marketing Management - Strategic Alliance - Three

Lesson Three - Managerial Marketing – Strategic Alliances

1. Discuss how the Corporate Mission is defined**** pg 65

A. What is our business?
B. Who is the customer?
C. What is of value to the customer?
D. What will our business be?
E. What should our business be?

2. Discuss the marketing strategy of the San Diego Zoo – pg 67
The San Diego Zoo needed to make going to the zoo more interesting. So they developed
educational classes including classeson how zoos affect the environment. This excellent R&D combined with Societal Concern has given the San Diego Zoo one of the highest rates of return on its investment dollars.

3. How are Strategic Business Units Established? Pg 68
Companies become associated with the slogans they create. This is a form of branding which adds recognition to the product. Examples would be: Nike: Just Do It, McDonalds: You Deserve a Break Today, Walmart: Low Prices, Every Day and Hertz: Leave the Driving to Us

4. Discuss the Superquinn marketing strategy – pg 63
Superquinn, a small market chain in Ireland, expanded its base by providing exceptional customer service and now has a larger market share for its type of business than any of its competitors in Ireland.

5. Discuss different types of growth and downsizing – pg 74-75
Companies usually consider the factor of rapid growth utilizing CURRENT PRODUCTS. After that primary consideration, they then consider NEW MARKETS for its CURRENT PRODUCTS. Thirdly, they then consider NEW PRODUCTS for its CURRENT MARKETS. Finally, they will consider NEW PRODUCTS for NEW MARKETS.
Downsizing occurs is performed to release needed resources or to reduce costs. It is a principle generally associated with poor business performance, but not in all instances.

6. Discuss the marketing strategy for Palm Computer and Topsy Tail – pg 67
They both use the strategy of outsourcing in order to reduce the bottom line, thereby increasing profits to the shareholders. Palm Computing also uses the low price strategy in combination with

the outsourcing.
7. Discuss the principle of Strategic Alliances**** – pg 81

Strategic Alliances fall into four main categories
A. Product or Service alliances – cross –licensing for mutual benefit
B. Promotional Alliances – companies agree to promote each other
C. Logistical Alliances – companies agree to warehouse each other
D. Pricing Collaborations – companies combine discounts if both are used

8. Discuss the marketing strategies of Apple Computer and Harley-Davidson.
Both companies have developed strong customer
base loyalties which creates a great deal of repeat business. This loyalty is gained by maintaining a very high level of customer service.

9. Define and discuss the contents of a Marketing Plan – pg 89
Components of a Marketing Plan include, but are not limited to:
Executive Summary and Table of Contents – A Brief Overview of the Proposal
Current Marketing Situation – current data on sales, costs, profits, competitors and others
Opportunity and Issue Analysis – Opportunities, Threats, Strengths and Weaknesses
Objectives – Marketing goals in sales volume, market share (pie), and profit
Marketing Strategy – Broad marketing approaches used to gain objectives
Action Programs – Special Marketing programs designed to achieve business objectives
Projected Profit and Loss Statement – Forecasts the plan's expected financial outcomes
Controls – Indicates how the plan will be monitored

ICA Homework – Essays – Lesson Three

Do your research first before making your move!

Write one paragraph on these questions

1. Why is the corporate mission statement important?
2. How are strategic business units established?
3. How are strategic alliances valuable?
4. How would you define a Marketing Plan?

Internet Resources for this lesson:

General Reference Material For All Content

http://www.askmrmovies.com

Strategic Alliances
www.1000ventures.com/.../strategic_alliances_main.html

Marketing Plans
www.mplans.com/

Tafero's Lesson Plan of Day - Marketing Management - Marketing Strategies - Four

Lesson Four - Marketing Strategies

1. Discuss the market research strategies of Rubbermaid and Motorola – pg 91

Both companies have missions that are highly focused on two primary goals: customer service and customer satisfaction.

2. Discuss the marketing strategy of Starbucks – pg 100
Starbucks uses a niche to add to its market development in the area of coffee house sales. Decidedly upscale in comparison to Dunking Donuts, it main competition, Starbucks has gained in market share because of its perceived quality.
3. Discuss the marketing strategy of Compaq – pg 110
Lost pie market share to Dell because of inadequate R&D. Copied the successful Direct Sales model of Dell and recaptured much of the market share it had lost previously.
4. Discuss the marketing strategy of Nike
Outsourcing
5. Discuss the Marketing Process.****- pg 112

A. Analyze Marketing Opportunities
B. R&D to select target markets
C. Design Strategies for those Markets
D. Organize, Implement and Control Campaign

6. Discuss the Marketing Strategies of Ascom Timplex and Montgomery Security – pg 124
Both companies employ a data driven strategy to gain an advantage and market share of the pie over their competitors.

7. Discuss how Parker-Hannifin and Ceoexpress have similar marketing strategies – pg 126
They both employ data driven R&D to gain an advantage over their competition.

8. Discuss the various approaches of Market Research**** - pg 131
A. Observational Research
B. Focus Group Research
C. Survey Research
D. Behavioral Research
E. Experimental Research

9. Describe how data from integrated marketing communications and marketing research evolve into information that is used for marketing/product planning and organizational decision-making******pgs 141, 350 and 583.

(A) Integrated Marketing Communications (583), which is a concept of marketing communications planning that recognizes the added value of a comprehensive plan, in combination with marketing research, generates substantial R&D data. The comprehensive plan includes, but is not limited to: the evaluation of advertising, direct response, sales promotion and public relations.
(B) This new data is then used to formulate new Marketing/Product Planning (350) strategy, which helps to prevent new product failure from occurring prematurely.
(C) The new data is then integrated with the Marketing Decision Support System (MDSS) (141) for additional uses by the Board of Trustees. Some components of MDSS include: collection ofdata, systems, tools, and techniques with supporting software and hardware. The average company uses this data at Board of Trustees meetings to consider future initiatives as well as to correct previous miscalculations.

ICA Homework – Essays – Lesson Four

Obviously, Batman did not do his research on the river.

Write one paragraph on each of these questions

1. Why is the Marketing Process important?
2. How do we perform Market Research?
3. How do Market Research goals differ?
4. How do Marketing Strategies differ?

Internet Resources for this lesson:

General Reference Material For All Content

Marketing Process
www.marketingmo.com/

Market Research
www.quickmba.com/marketing/research/

Tafero's Lesson Plan of Day - Marketing Management - The Social-Cultural Environment - Five

Lesson Five -The Social-Cultural Environment

1. Discuss the marketing strategy of Colgate-Palmolive
By using substantial R&D, Colgate was able to
make significantgains in the market share pie of the
international toothpaste market.
2. Discuss the marketing strategy of Volkswagen.
Volkswagen already has the advantage of being a German car
company. Germans, for one reason or another, are perceived by
asignificant percentage of the pie to be superior in development
of engines, but it was their customer loyalty that gained them a
niche in the highly competitive auto market.

3. Discuss the marketing strategy of Sears.
Sears uses a very sensible marketing strategy of matching its
local inventories to the demographics of whatever city they are
selling in. For example, they will market items within a Hispanic
community that their R&D has shown are attractive to Hispanic
customers. They follow the same strategy internationally.

4. Discuss the similar marketing strategies of Absolut and Boreal
Ski Area – pg 166

They both employ the strategy of creating a niche by segmenting specified groups. Absolut targets gays and Boreal Ski Area targets Chinese living on the West Coast of the US.

5. Discuss the marketing strategy of Kinko's. – pg 168
Kinko's uses outsourcing as its primary attraction to customers. Customers of Kinko's are too busy to spend the necessary hours to prepare paper presentations to various attendees of a meeting, so Kinko's does this and a myriad of other office tasks for them for a reasonable price. This has created almost a monopolistic niche for Kinko's in the office outsourcing area.

6. Discuss the unfortunate fate of Encyclopedia Britannica – pg 171
Encyclopedia Britannica became obsolete as soon as users of computers began to figure out they could download the entire contents of Encyclopedia Britannica on just one disc. Why pay over a thousand dollars for something that you can get for less than ten dollars?

7. Discuss the marketing strategy of Wellman - pg 174
Wellman uses the strategy of social concern for its marketing efforts. Cashing in on the recycling craze, Wellman is both making money and gives the perception that it is very concerned about the environment.

8. Discuss the marketing strategy of Publishers Clearinghouse – pg 174
Simply put, Publishers Clearinghouse considers the public to be a very large group of morons who can easily be fooled into spending money for the miniscule chance that they might become rich overnight in a lottery. This company has been fined and paid 16 million dollars to its supposed "Sweepstakes" entries for not being totally honest about their chances of winning. The lesson here is that scamming your customer base is not really a good way to gain customer loyalty, but it is a good way to wind up in jail.

.

9. Discuss the variables of Social-Cultural Environment***** – pg 175
A. People have views of themselves
B. People have views of others
C. People have views of organizations
D. People have views of society
E. People have views of nature
F. People have views of the Universe

ICA Homework – Essays – Lesson Five

Here is a challenging social environment

Write a paragraph on each of these questions:

1. How can we learn from the Encyclopedia Britannica fiasco?
2. Why was Volkswagen so successful in their marketing campaign?
3. How did Kinko's make enormous profits on their assets?
4. How do views differ in the Social-Cultural Environment?

Internet Resources for this lesson:

General Reference Material For All Content

http://www.askmrmovies.com

Social-Cultural Environment

www.slideshare.net/

Volkswagen Marketing

www.autointell.com/.../volkswagen/vw.../volkswagen.../volkswag18.htm

Tafero's Lesson Plan of Day - Marketing Management - Consumer Segments - Six

Lesson Six - Consumer Segments

1. Discuss the similar marketing strategies of Whirlpool Corporation and Net-Temps – pg 183
Both companies perform extensive research and development for their products. This R&D is data driven for Net-Temps while Whirlpool seeks a particular segments like men and kids to expand its market share pie in washer and dryer machines.

2. Discuss the similarities of marketing for Abercrombie and Fitchand Levi Strauss – pg 187
Both companies target specific groups for their products. The segmentation of Abercrombie and Fitch is the college crowd, while the segmentation of Levi Strauss is the high school to college crowd. Almost, but not quite the same segment. Abercrombie and Fitch have a decided niche in the college market, while Levi Strausshas a much wider appeal over many other segments.

3. Discuss the marketing strategy of Edmunds.com – pg 203
This web site provides excellent mediation for buying autos and related services. They are both objective and considered a great source of information. They have created a niche for themselves in this market.

4. Discuss the sources for information******* - pg 204
A. Personal Sources
B. Commercial Sources
C. Public Sources
D. Experiential Sources

5. Discuss how buyers vary by product – pg 205
Cameras – sharpness, speed, size and price

Hotels – Location, cleanliness, atmosphere and price
Mouthwash – Color, effectiveness, taste and price
Tires – Safety, Tread Life, ride quality and price

6. Discuss the marketing strategy of Avon – pg 208
Avon products have added benefit. One of its skin oils accidently happens to be a great insect repellent. The company cashed in on this through R&D and added another layer of benefit. The same product also offered 15 level sunscreen protection! (Skin-So-Soft Bath Oil)

7. Discuss the stages of the decision process of consumers in the health field – pg 209
Consumers in the health field go through these five stages:
A. Precontemplation – not recognizing problem or need to change
B. Contemplation – Seriously thinking about the problem and the need to change
C. Preparation – Making a plan to make changes
D. Action – Actually making the change
E. Maintenance – Maintaining the change

8. Discuss the factor of obsolescence for items like the Blackberry and Sony Walkman – pg 212
These two products have been overtaken by competitors like Iphone, which accomplishes two major tasks much better than Blackberry and Ipods which is a much more personalized form of music entertainment than is Sony Walkman. Now these two items are only sold in third world countries.

ICA Homework – Essays – Lesson Six

Cell phones have now become indispensible

Internet Resources for this lesson:

General Reference Material For All Content

Consumer Buying Habits

Business Information Sources

Tafero's Lesson Plan of Day - Marketing Management - The Business Buying Process - Seven

Lesson Seven – The Business Buying Process

1. Discuss the marketing strategy for Cisco - 217
Cisco has built a strong customer base directly related to excellent quality and service. It costs a bit more than other companies in the same business, but it has a better reputation than those other companies.

2. Discuss the marketing strategy of Blue Shield of California – pg 217
Blue Shield of California has increased its market share of the pie due to its superior tech driven database and R&D. This data gives this company an advantage over its competitors.

3. Discuss the marketing strategy of Cutler-Hammer – pg 218
Cutler-Hammer uses the team-sales approach in segmentation. They divide their customers for electrical equipment into geographical and regional sections. Then they divide up their

sales force the same way so they can better serve each region and geographical area.

4. Discuss the marketing strategy of Ford – pg 220
Ford has eliminated the production aspect of its business. It has outsourced all of its production to outside vendors who offer the cheapest price for mass-produced parts. This generally is a price-driven, low quality strategy that should translate into very low prices for the consumer, but in reality Ford still tries to charge close to the same prices of its competitors who use a higher standard of quality for their components. The Ford company used to stand for quality and service. It has spent that goodwill with cheap parts and low quality, thereby losing customer loyalty. Not a very good strategy in my opinion.

5. Discuss the participants in business buying process – pg 221****
A. Initiators – those who request something to purchase
B. Users – Those who will use the product or service
C. Influencers – Those who influence the buying decision
D. Deciders – Those who actually decide to buy
E. Approvers – Those who authorize the proposed actions of the decider
F. Buyers – People who have the formal authority to buy
G. Gatekeepers – People who have the power to prevent sellers from reaching the buyer

6. Discuss the marketing strategy of Campbell Soup Company - 230
Campbell Soup uses extremely strong quality control measures for all of its products and distribution. This provides Campbell to use the just-in-time method of supplying their stores in order for inventory to be timely and storage to be minimal. Of course there are always minimal risks to the just-in-time method such as shortages of various items. But when used correctly, it is a money-saving device.

7. Discuss the marketing strategy of Hewlett-Packard – pg 232

Hewlett-Packard uses the "trusted advisor" role that many tech companies get when they do business with companies not very well steeped in tech. Some customers want complete technical assistance (which costs a great deal more money), while other more tech-savvy companies merely want some tech that works well without too much advice.

8. Discuss the marketing strategy of Advanced Travel Management – pg 232
Advanced Travel Management uses high quality of customer service in order to gain a niche in the upper end of the Travel Management business. It caters to upper end clients with sophisticated needs who want fast quality service. They are able to charge much more than the average travel services because they provide this superior service.

9. Discuss the marketing strategy of Lincoln Electric – pg 233
Lincoln Electric sells its products with the following promise: It will match or beat any of its competitor's prices or it will refund the difference in price. This is a good strategy that works well because it gives the impression that you are always getting the lowest price (which is not true). You will get the lowest price some of the time, but if you have the reputation of matching the lowest price, a buyer usually does not do the R&D to find lower prices that may exist elsewhere. In effect, you are losing the rebate if you do not do your research properly. Lincoln will not do your research for you and will charge you the extra money unless you find the data yourself. A very clever approach.

ICA Homework – Essays – Lesson Seven

This is NOT Bill Gates and Microsoft….and the other guy is NOT Apple.

Internet Resources for this lesson:

General Reference Material For All Content

http://www.askmrmovies.com

Software Wars

www.mshiltonj.com/software_wars/current/

Microsoft vs Google

www.pcworld.com/.../google_vs_microsoft_its_going_to_get_worse_in_2010.html

Tafero's Lesson Plan of Day - Marketing Management - Competition - Eight

Lesson 8 - Competitive Forces

1. Discuss Competitive Forces**** - 242
A. Threat of Intense Segment Rivalry – too many competitors make a segment unattractive
B. Threat of New Entrants – Just when you think you have the market to yourself, someone new comes in and upsets the apple cart.
C. Threat of Substitute Products – Like ants at a picnic, substitute products can eat into your market share pie before you know it.
D. Threat of Growing Buyer Strength – You don't want your buyers getting as much leverage as you have or you become squeezed.

2. Discuss the obsolescence of Encyclopedia Britannica and Palm Pilot – pg 243
Encyclopedia Britannica has been replaced by an eight year old child who can download its entire content in ten minutes for a

cost of one dollar. Palm Pilot has been blown away by the current Iphone from Apple and newer products will make it even more obsolete. Both of these products can now only be sold in third world countries.

3. Discuss the marketing strategy of Selfridges – pg 255
R&D discovered they had lost market share with the younger crowd, so the store refurbished its younger crowd selections and they regained a significant portion of their loss.

4. Discuss the marketing strategies of Michelin Tires and Gillette – pg 256
The Michelin Tire company uses the dangerous strategy of scamming their customers into using their tires up more quickly so they can sell them more new ones. Not a wise path. Gillette Razors and Blades sections use the same scamming technique. It has worked for them because of the relative laziness of the consumer.

5. Discuss the extremely good fortune of Johnson and Johnson - pg 258
Johnson and Johnson had ridiculously good luck when it went into the Stint market and practically controlled the entire sector. Eventually, its completion eroded away well over 90% of their pie. This would appear to be bad luck, but stints were found to be defective for the use of preventing heart attacks and the class action suit that followed only cost Johnson and Johnson about 10% of the settlement instead of the 90% they would have paid had they maintained their market share. Now THAT is really good luck.

6. Discuss the marketing strategy of Heublein – pg 259
Hueblein found a clever way to defend its market share of the pie from Wolfschmidt, a competing vodka. It raised its price by one dollar and took the profits to make another product to undercut Wolfschmidt in price.

7. Discuss the marketing strategy of Goodyear – pg 259
Goodyear employed the strategy of horizontal expansion to ward off the fierce competition of the tire market in the 90s.

8. Discuss the marketing strategy of Chrysler in the 1990s – pg 259

Lee Iacocca of Chrysler made a pre-emptive strike on the competition by announcing that the popular minivan would be joined by a less expensive version to be put in production. This thwarted any competition from profiting from making a cheaper version of the minivan.

9. Discuss the marketing strategy of Walmart**** – pg 260

Walmart already had the leading market share of the pie in non-food products by 1998. It also had very large physical plants built previous to that year. It was a relatively easy transformation to a food-non-food combo from the primarily non-food predecessors. The competition in food markets have suffered great losses in the market share pie and have been forced to slash prices and profits to try and keep up.

ICA Homework – Essays – Lesson Eight

Don't we all dream of having the perfect wedding like this one in Walmart?

Internet Resources for this lesson:

General Reference Material For All Content

http://www.askmrmovies.com

Walmart Marketing Success

www.sbinformation.about.com/cs/.../a/impactplan.htm

Competitive Forces

www.quickmba.com/strategy/porter.shtml

Tafero's Lesson Plan of Day - Marketing Management - Market Segments - Nine

Lesson 9 – Market Segments

1. Discuss the similarities of marketing strategy among Hallmark, Estee Lauder, and Progressive Corporation – pg 280
All three companies target specific segments of the population for campaigns: Hallmark targets Blacks, Hispanics and young women, Estee Lauder has three separate lines for three different age groups of women, and Progressive targets bad drivers.

2. Discuss Useful Market Segments**** pg 286
A. Measurable – size, purchasing power
B. Substantial – large and profitable
C. Accessible – can be reached and served
D. Differentiable – must be completely different from other segments
E. Actionable – effective program can put into action right away

3. Discuss Pillsbury strategy- pg 287
Pillsbury is data driven and uses R&D with tech to gain market share

4. Discuss the marketing strategy of Sega – pg 289
Sega seeks customer loyalty from cutting edge tech. It is trying to widen segments.

5. Discuss the marketing strategy of Eddie Bauer – pg 289
Eddie Bauer uses in-house advertising on large plasma TVs while customers are shopping. This technique has proved to increase sales in all outlets.

6. Discuss the marketing strategy of Ivillage.com – pg 290
Ivillage.com targets the segment for females. Beside the baby boomer segment, it targets young mothers.

7. Discuss the marketing strategy of Bank of America – pg 293
Bank of America provides a high level of service to its customers, thereby justifying its higher fees for its services. It has also recently created a strategic alliance with the Construction China Bank to wire money for a low fee in both directions.

8. Discuss IBM marketing strategy – pg 297
Has been successful in targeting large corporate accounts. It also targets specific segments such as women, blacks, Hispanics, gays and Asians. However, they have failed in the computer market and had to sell their interests in that area to Lenovo of China, who has vigorously, attacked both the domestic and international markets for computers.

9. Discuss the practices of BB&T – pg 297
BB&T was engaged in illegal activity during 2008. It kept secret files on some of its customers when those customers were involved romantically with any of its employees. The fear of embezzlement or mismanagement of funds was the reason for the files, but that did not change the fact that they were blatantly illegal and violated the civil rights of the customers and others mentioned in the files. The US government has not yet stepped in to stop this practice, but a substantial lawsuit or two by private individuals mentioned in the files might be enough for them to subsist in this practice.

ICA Homework – Essays – Lesson Nine

Each Sales Manager in a company fights for his or her share of the budget

Write one paragraph on each of these essay questions

1. Why is market segmentation information useful?
2. Why is customer loyalty important and how can it be exploited?
3. How did Bank of American and the China Construction Bank gain a competitive edge on their rivals?
4. Why did companies like IBM and ATT lose substantial market shares?

Internet Resources for this lesson:

General Reference Material for All Content

http://www.askmrmovies.com

Market Segmentation

Bank of America Marketing

Tafero's Lesson Plan of Day - Marketing Management - Focus Groups - Ten

Lesson 10 – Focus Groups

1. Discuss the strategy of Home Depot – pg 310
Quality sales staff with practical experience gives Home Depot an edge in hardware. Quality is assured and loyal customers do not mind paying a few dollars more for the privilege.

2. Discuss the concept of positioning****-pg 311
A. Attribute Positioning – size, experience
B. Competitor Positioning – better than the competition quantified
C. Product Leader Positioning – Best product in the field
D. Quality or Price Positioning – Highest quality or lowest price in the field

3. Discuss the DiGiorno Pizza marketing strategy – pg 314
Digiorno markets itself the same as delivered pizza, thereby removing itself from its frozen pizza competition. Differentiation that works with a slogan, "It's not delivery, it's Digiorno!" Another slogan that was successful in pizza was "Better Ingredients, Better Pizza" by Papa Johns. Unfortunately, some franchises of theirs in China did not live up to the slogan..

4. Discuss the marketing strategy of General Motors – pg 318
GM uses the Onstar system which provides customers with a very real sense of security in case of an emergency. This added benefit also serves a differentiation from the competition.

5. Discuss the strategy of Cisco – pg 320
Cisco relies on its database for FAQ and is data driven for customer support.

6. Discuss the marketing strategy of Apple Computers – pg 321
Apple uses style to sell some of their products. Apple also has some superior internal engineering to Windows and easier navigation. Their only drawback is that they have a very small piece of the tech pie. Stores stock well over 90% of windows products. Innovation is the only edge Apple has in the tech market.

7. Discuss the marketing strategy of Black and Decker – pg 321
Black and Decker features superior design for tools. Added to the sturdy composition of all primary Black and Decker tools, the customer receives a very high level of quality for a very reasonable price. This creates a positive value for the customer. They primarily follow the Walmart principle in marketing (and are carried by all of their stores)

8. Discuss the marketing strategy of Rite-Aid – pg 324
Rite-aid has cleverly added strong customer support via its pharmacy build-up and bringing back the good old days when you could go to your pharmacist instead of a doctor to get medical advice.

9. Discuss the marketing strategy of Yahoo – pg 333
Founded in 1994 by web-surfing grad students, Yahoo started as a search engine. By 1998 it was worth over 9 Billion dollars. When the tech stocks crashed at the end of the decade, Yahoo lost over 75% of its worth. It has the strategy of taking current losses in the hope of future profits. A risky venture at best. Yahoo has been annihilated in the market by Google and Bing and will continue to lose market share for the rest of the decade. A weak attempt at creating content with Associated Content, a subsidiary of Yahoo, has resulted in some reclamation of the pie, but when Google and Bing eventually enter the content competition, Yahoo might go out of business for good.

ICA Homework – Essays – Lesson Ten

Positioning is Extremely Important

Write a paragraph on each of these essay questions:

1. How did Yahoo lose its market share?
2. Why does Black and Decker have a sound marketing strategy?
3. Why is the marketing strategy of Apple dangerous?
4. Why are the concepts of positioning important?

Internet Resources for this lesson:

General Reference Material For All Content

Yahoo's Failure

Positioning

Tafero's Lesson Plan of Day - Marketing Management - Why Most Businesses Fail- Eleven

Lesson 11- Why Most Businesses Fail (80% of all businesses fail within 3 yrs)

Source: Wharton School of Business, Penn U.

1. Why do new products fail***** pg 350
A. Product not well-designed
B. Product not advertised correctly
C. Product Overpriced
D. Product fails to get distribution
E. Competitors crush it

2. Discuss Proctor and Gamble – pg 356
Outstanding R&D equals almost foolproof products that reach the market

3. Discuss Lego Group – pg 358
Strict Marketing segmentation for children to meet the following criteria:

A. Will children learn while having fun?
B. Does the product have the Lego look?
C. High Quality Standards?
D. Will parents approve?
E. Does it Stimulate Creativity?

4. Discuss Gadd International – pg 360
Gadd has developed software similar to Sim City that simulates the focus group and survey experience as well as experimental research. Wonderful data-driven SW tool.

5. Discuss National Semiconductor – pg 360
Uses the mediation technique with substantial database for the purposes of tracking customer searches for tech items which then in turn creates more data. Very clever.

6. Discuss Boeing – pg 366
Boeing uses digital design which saves millions of dollars. In addition, it uses its database to share with suppliers so they can custom-make parts for Boeings specifications at a lower price, thereby saving millions of more dollars. R&D is king.

7. Discuss the marketing testing technique of Apple Computer – pg 368
It is important for Apple R&D testers to create scenarios that are both realistic and far more strenuous on the product than would be expected from average use. Pepsi, mayo, and car-baking are included in the tests.

8. Discuss the marketing strategy of Sony Pictures – pg 372
Sony spent $125 million on Godzilla, but spent over $200 million in sales promotion. The cost of sales promotion was defrayed by over $150 million coming in for licensing marketing partners like Taco Bell and sellers of tee shirts, backpacks and other promotional items. The strategy paid off and Sony made well over the $175 total million it laid out for the film.

9. Discuss Red Bull – pg 377
After success in Europe, Red Bull started small in small local markets in California and then spread out to San Francisco and

an all-out assault on big American cities. A good example of not wasting a lot of money all at one time on massive national marketing campaigns.

ICA Homework – Essays – Lesson Eleven

Why did this monster fail in marketing?

Write one paragraph on each of these essays:

1. How did Sony Pictures successfully market Godzilla? (this also answers the above question as to why Molten Man Thing failed.
2. Why do four out of five businesses fail within three years?
3. Why is the National Semiconductor marketing strategy clever?
4. How does Boeing stay on top in the mass market for planes?

Internet Resources for this lesson:

General Reference Material For All Content

http://www.askmrmovies.com

Percentage of All Business Failures

www.gaebler.com › ... › Articles on Business Failure

National Semiconductor Marketing

www.national.com/news/item/0,1735,997,00.html

Tafero's Lesson Plan of Day - Marketing Management - Branding - Twelve

Lesson 12 - Branding

Famous Logos

1. Discuss the global strategy of the NBA – pg 384
The NBA markets its games in over 200 countries in 42 languages. It also creates partnering deals with other global marketers such asCoca-Cola, Reebok, and McDonalds. Unlike Major League Baseball, which is only played in the Americas and Asia, or the NHL, which is only played in North America and Europe, or the NFL, which is only played in the United States, the NBA is international and is equal to or even higher-rated than soccer as an international sport.

2. Discuss General Electric's strategy for creating bigger profits – pg 400
General Electric decided not to go for more MS pie. It went, instead, to its top 100 customers and asked them what was important they could improve upon. This R&D created greater customer loyalty and also created greater efficiency for both GE and all of their customers resulting in a large increase in profits.

3. Discuss the Branding strategy of Virgin Atlantic Airlines – pg 409
Virgin takes quality to the extreme. It provides every creature comfort known to man, but the price is very high. Rich people don't worry about the price. Very segmented Branding.

4. Discuss what constitutes a Brand**** – pg 418
A. Attributes – Mercedes suggests expensive, well-engineered, high-prestige autos
B. Benefits – Quality cars like Mercedes actually last much

longer than most cars and can cost about the same as buying two inferior cars over the same time period.

C. Values – Buying a Mercedes says you are a person who wants performance and prestige

D. Culture – Mercedes represents German culture, which in turn represents the best engineering in the world

E. Personality – A Mercedes generally represents a no-nonsense individual who is a high level manager of some type.

F. User – The Mercedes user is generally an older executive man in his fifties rather than a younger female secretary in her twenties or thirties.

5. Discuss the marketing strategy of Volvo cars – pg 420
The Volvo Brand stands for safety. The segment of the population that is safety-conscious will automatically be drawn to Volvos at some point because all of their advertising goes toward that segment.

6. Discuss the failure of Pets.com – pg 421
Pets.com did everything right but develop a marketable product from R&D. This caused them to go bankrupt.

7. Discuss the branding strategy of Virgin – pg 423
The Virgin line of companies follows the same pattern as Virgin Atlantic Airways. Quality to the nth degree. The owner of all these companies, Richard Branson, rivals Bill Gates as one of the richest and most successful men in the world.

8. Discuss the branding strategy for AOL – pg429
AOL was associated with the browser for the tech-handicapped. Unfortunately for AOL, the vast majority of the United States and the rest of the world that were tech-handicapped and don't know the difference between a browser and other software functions, eventually became much more sophisticated and started downloading free browsers. It had created brand distinction because it has distributed its ridiculously easy set-up disc to practically every person in the United States for free. Those who try it are usually first-time computer users and are afraid to change browsers for a number of reasons. Some users thought they would lose their email addresses if they change browsers.

AOL mail is free and you can keep your email address and still use another free browser like Firefox, Google Chrome, or MSN.

9. Discuss the importance of labeling**** – pg 437
A. Labels identify the product or brand
B. Labels describe the product; who made it, where, when, how and contents
C. Labels are designed to attract the buyer
D. Some labels are misleading; percentages of ingredients help

ICA Homework – Essays – Lesson Twelve

This is a prime example of branding. We all know who this is.

Write a paragraph for the following essay questions:

1. Why is branding important to a company?
2. Why is labeling an important factor in marketing?
3. Why did AOL lose almost all of its market share?
4. How has the NBA successfully marketed itself internationally?

Internet Resources for this lesson:

General Reference Material For All Content

http://www.askmrmovies.com

Branding
www.entrepreneur.com › Sales & Marketing

The NBA Marketing Strategy

www.allbusiness.com/marketing...brand.../4689416-1.html

Tafero's Lesson Plan of Day - Marketing Management - Pricing - Thirteen

Lesson 13 - Pricing and Cost

Wholesale Cost Of One Big Mac as of 2010: $1.21

1. Discuss Acme Construction Supply – pg 444
Acme delivers 24 hours a day. This added benefit to customer service provides them with a competitive edge and customer loyalty.

2. Discuss Dot-Com Providers – pg 445
These various service companies provide pay-as-you-go online advice that is paid by the minute. You can get ANY service in ANY field via this method (doctors, lawyers, child counseling, adult counseling, business advice etc).

3. Discuss USPS – pg 449
The United States Postal Service used to be a joke; now it competes and often beats UPS and Fed-Ex because of its price strategy while maintaining an acceptable level of service. The second-day priority mail is a good example of its quality.

4. Discuss Schwab.com – pg 451
It used to be very expensive to buy and sell stocks before the computer age. Transactions would cost, on the average, between $50 and $100 each. Now Schwab completes the exact same transactions online for $10, an 80 to 90% reduction. This price-driven strategy has virtually erased the need for physical stockbrokers. The level of service may not be as high as

premium stockbrokers, but it is good enough for those who trade in high volume or have an idea of what they are doing already.

5. Discuss factors to consider in setting price policy*****- pg 473
A. Create a Price Objective
B. Do R&D to determine Demand
C. Estimate the Total Cost of your Product
D. Do R&D to determine your competitor's costs, prices and marketing strategy
E. Select a pricing Method – Cost+competitor's price+demand
F. Select a temporary Final Price- ALL Prices are temporary.
6. Discuss an example of Temporary Pricing – pg 474
Sony is a good example of Temporary Pricing. New tech is always more expensive when it is new to the market and then gradually goes down in price until a new technology comes to the market. Sony sold their 1990 HDTVs in Japan for $43,000. Then, by 1993, they were able to reduce the price for the same item to $6,000. By 2001, the same item was selling for less than $2000 and in late 2008, you can buy one for less than $500. Refinement of Technology and competition will constantly erode the original price for innovative tech items.

7. How do we establish Cost?****** - pg 478
Establishing cost is a classic example of the pie. Cost Accounting is basically analyzing all the parts of the pie to see which parts are causing prices to go up or down. For example, if you are selling sugar and the total cost of a pound of sugar is 87 cents; there are numerous variables that go into the cost at 87 cents such as:
A. Average cost of raw sugar acquisition – 23 cents
B. Average cost of raw sugar storage – 4 cents
C. Average cost of refining raw sugar to finished sugar – 2 cents
D. Average cost of finished sugar storage – 4 cents
E. Average cost of transport of finished sugar – 8 cents
F. Average cost of selling one pound of refined sugar – 5 cents
Total Cost of One Pound of Sold Refined Sugar – 46 cents;
Wholesale Selling Price: 87 cents
Net Profit 87-46 = 41 cents per pound of refined sugar times X amount of tons = total profit

Raising the price or lowering the cost of refinement will result in higher profits in the pie.

8. Discuss how Dell establishes a pricing strategy. – pg 488
Dell does R&D on its demand and the demand of its competitors, the total cost of producing each product of their own and their competitors products and raises or lowers the price of each product according to variations of these numbers.

9. Discuss Discriminatory Pricing. – pg 491
Some companies charge different prices for the same quantity of the same product sold in different places. American foods in China, for example, sometimes sell for 2x to 3x the price sold for in the US.

ICA Homework – Essays – Lesson Thirteen

We can learn a lot about pricing and cost from surfing.......on the internet, not here.

Write a paragraph on each one of these essay questions:

1. Why is pricing crucial to business success?
2. Why is cost essential to pricing?
3. How can an online company put a marketplace (brick and motar) company out of business?
4. Why is surfing an extremely important part of research and development?

Internet Resources for this lesson:

General Reference Material For All Content

http://www.askmrmovies.com

Pricing Strategy

www.netmba.com/marketing/pricing/

Costing Strategy

www.cga-pdnet.org/en-CA/pd/tk/ma/pcs

Tafero's Lesson Plan of Day - Marketing Management - Managing Distribution - Fourteen

Lesson 14 – Managing Distribution

The United States of Wal-Mart (these are just super-centers)

1. Discuss People's com bank – pg 508
People's .com bank added a marketspace to a marketplace in 1995 and gave customers added value and service. They also do same-day email answering services for their customers.

2. Discuss Chiodo Candy Company – pg 513
Lost Pie to Brach Candy for supermarket shelf space. Company did R@D on club and warehouse stores to replace the supermarkets. Clubs and warehouse stores wanted bigger packages of candy to wholesale out. Chiodo R&D developed a two pound tub of penny candy that began to move briskly. A good case study of how to regain some pie.

3. Discuss the sales channels of Disney Videos – pg 514
Disney sells its videos through five different channels:
A. Video rental stores
B. Disney stores
C. Retail Outlets – Walmart etc
D. Online Retailers – Amazon
E. Disney Online stores

4. Discuss the failure of the Japanese company – Epson – pg 517
Epson had a fairly decent piece of the pie for printers. They decided (without any R&D) that they would enter the computer market. They were destroyed and the cost of the venture negatively impacted their pie for printers. Lesson: Look before you leap.

5. Discuss methods of managing distributors**** - pg 518

A. Coercive- manufacturer threatens to withdraw product if distributor fails to cooperate 100%. Effective, but heavy-handed and sometimes self-destructive.
B. Reward – manufacturer rewards distributors for meeting various quotas. Generally more effective than coercion, but has it own pitfalls. A dog that gets a biscuit for doing one trick will want a biscuit for doing all other tricks or it may not do them at all.
C. Contractual power – the manufacturer requires the distributor to fulfill all elements of the contract with coercion or extra reward. This method is very solid.
D. Expert power – the manufacturer has special knowledge that the distributor wishes to stay in the loop for. This power can vanish in one day, so it is not the most dependable strategy. However it is useful in certain situations.
E. Reputational power – distributors are so impressed by the manufacturer's reputation (Microsoft, Walmart) that they perform at a very high level without A, B, C or D.
F. Any combination of A-E.

6. Discuss the strategy of Apple adding a channel to its distribution. – pg 521
Apple opened its own retail outlets in 2001. This upset its current

distributors, but Apple explained it already had a marketspace that sold 25% of its product online and needed physical plants to store and sell that part of its market. (Personally, if I were a distributor, I would not have bought into this explanation).

7. Discuss the marketing strategy of the Gap – pg 523
The Gap has cleverly established three channels for its product. A higher priced channel, Banana Republic and a lower priced channel called Old Navy. This is protection from competitors who try to out-quality or outprice the Gap's middle of the road prices and quality.

8. Discuss how some companies have reconciled their marketplaces with marketspaces – pg 528
A. Talbots- uses a catalog to augment its stores
B. Liberty Mutual – uses its online capacities to feed its physical company space
C. Avon – offers onlines sales as an augmentation to its sales staff
D. JC Penny – offers online coupons that can be used in its marketplace stores
E. Gibson Guitars – involves local marketplaces for its accessories through the internet

9. Discuss Exclusivity in Distribution – pg 530
This method of distribution is favorable to the distributor, but sometimes limits the Manufacturer. These types of arrangements should only be made if the distributor can deliver better-than-average results that would be achieved by have numerous distributors.

ICA Homework – Essays – Lesson Fourteen

Some Serious Distribution

Write a paragraph for each of these essay questions:

1. Why is efficient distribution essential to any business?
2. Why is Walmart a top model for distribution?
3. How can poor distribution subvert even the best products?
4. How do marketspaces and marketplaces compare for distribution?

Internet Resources for this lesson:

General Reference Material For All Content

http://www.askmrmovies.com

Distribution Strategies

www.capv.com/public/Content/MRD/.../distributionstrategies.html

Walmart Distribution
www.helium.com › Business › International Business & Trade

Tafero's Lesson Plan of Day - Marketing Management - Wholesale and Advertising - Fifteen

Lesson 15 – Wholesale Marketing Decisions and Advertising

Wholesale Agricultural Warehouse

1. Discuss Walmart – pg 539
Walmart franchises follow the following simple marketing strategies:
A. Listen to Customers
B. Treat Employees as Partners
C. Push for Lower Prices from Suppliers
D. Keep Expenses down
E. Use the best databases available

2. Discuss General Electric Marketing Strategy – pg 541
GE provides models for its products rather than stocking many of its products in any number of stores. The advantage of this system is that it limits the cost of stockpiling inventory at each store. The major drawback of this system is that the customer does not get the product on the same day that it buys it.

3. Discuss how the store design of Kohl's allows it to gain a competitive edge – pg 543
Kohl's designed its store to have the shape of a racetrack for the convenience of shoppers to shop for everything they want quickly. This innovative design yields much more sales per square foot than any of its competitors including Target and Dillards.

4. Discuss the Wholesaler Marketing Decisions*****pg 549
A. Target Market – Who will you be wholesaling to?
B. Product Assortment and Services – Design your line and service for your line
C. Estimate Your Wholesales Prices – General rule of thumb is about 20% mark-up or you may be undersold by competition.
D. Create Sales Promotions For Your Line – Individual and Team sellers can create their own promotions in addition to formal company promotions.
E. Warehousing and Placement Decisions – Where will you keep your Inventory? How will you get it to your retailers?

5. Discuss the marketing change of the American Cancer Society (ACS)- pg 570
After an unsuccessful ad campaign to prevent skin cancer from excessive tanning by using sun block 15 by using the slogan "Save Your Life!", the ACS changed its campaign by saying sun block 15 would allow you MORE time in the sun AND get a better tan. The second campaign worked very well. This is a good example of how to turn around an unsuccessful ad campaign.

6. Discuss the marketing strategy of BMW – pg 572
Adding to the advantage of BMW's reputation for German Engineering, the company decided to recruit Hollywood celebrities driving BMW in film clips. Customers saw the Hollywood stars driving BMWs and they wanted to be like their idols, so they inquired about buying more BMWs. The campaign was a success.

7. Discuss Amazon.com and the power of the internet – pg 574
Amazon.com has been at the forefront of providing excellent customer service on the internet. This has translated into good word of mouth advertising for the company. Its founder, Jeff Bezos reminded his workers that good customer service will gain another five customers, but poor service to a tech-oriented customer could cause bad word of mouth from 5000 to 50000 potential customers.

8. Discuss how sales promotion or advertising budgets are created***** – pg 577
A. Haphazard guessing without any R&D – The vast majority of companies use this method, believe it or not. They take what they can afford and spend it on ads HOPING it will bring profits on a certain product they are promoting.
B. Percentage of Sales Method – A much more sensible and reliable method of budgeting for your ad campaigns. 2% of sales seems to be the general rule for this method.
C. Spend the Same as Your Competitor(s) – This is another haphazard method used by many companies. If your competition is spending 5% or more on advertising, then according to this method, you should be matching that percentage.
D. Objective and Task Method – This complicated method is

seldom used because the cost of implementing it is almost as expensive as the advertising itself in some cases. It takes every aspect of the campaign and breaks it down in micro-managing components. Implementing this method is difficult, at best.

9. Discuss promotional tools***** - pg 580
A. Advertising – budgets can vary, but you must advertise
B. Sales Promotion – coupons, contests, special sales
C. Pubic Relations and Publicity – make strategic alliances with city and local groups
D. Personal Selling – establish a close relationship with the customer
E. Direct Marketing – direct mail, telemarketing (not recommended), internet (recommended)

ICA Homework – Essays – Lesson Fifteen

Voted Number 1 Annoying Ad of All Time – Vote here

Write a paragraph for each of these essay questions:

1. Why is Sales promotion essential for a business?
2. Why is Advertising essential for a business?
3. Why are Wholesale Marketing Decisions crucial?
4. How would you promote your own business?

Internet Resources for this lesson:

General Reference Material For All Content

http://www.askmrmovies.com

Sales Promotion Strategies

www.smallbusinessbible.org/salespromotionstrategy.html

Wholesale Marketing Decisions
www.mba.zainbooks.com/.../marketing/wholesaler-marketing-decisions_marke...

Tafero's Lesson Plan of Day - Marketing Management - Media Ads - Sixteen

Lesson 16 – Media Ads and Consumer Feedback

Social Media is almost as effective as High-Cost Media

1. Discuss advertising objectives*****- pg 591
A. Informative Advertising – introduce new products
B. Persuasive Advertising – uses competition to sell your product
C. Reminder Advertising – stimulation of repeat customer impulse
D. Reinforcement Advertising – You made the right choice ads

2. Discuss the marketing strategy of Ethical Funds – pg 598
Ethical Funds is a fund management company that carefully avoids investing in companies that may have ethical problems such as: weapons, smoking, nuclear power, unfair employment practices, poor environmental practices, and companies associated with dictatorships. Their business has grown from 100 Mil to 2 Billion in 10 years.

3. Discuss the advantages and disadvantages of the following media ads****: - pg 601
A. Newspapers – good local coverage---short life
B. TV – high attention rate ----high cost
C. Direct Mail – selectivity-----high cost
D. Radio ----selectivity ----low attention rate
E. Magazines –long life----lead time too long
F. Outdoor (Bus) –low cost----limited selectivity
G. Phone Book – low cost-----high competition
H. Newsletters ----high selectivity ---high cost potential**
I. Brochures----flexible----high cost potential**
J. Telephone---personal----high cost
K. Internet----high selectivity, low cost----low number of users in some places

4. Discuss Pizza Hut – pg 606
Budgets double the usual advertising expense for its franchisers (4%). National Advertising is efficient, but does not address local franchise needs.

5. What are some questions to ask for consumer feedback?****- pg 607
A. What is the main message you got from this ad?
B. What does the ad want you to know, do or believe?
C. Will this ad influence you?
D. What worked well in the ad; and what worked poorly?
E. How does the ad make you feel?
F. Where does this message make the greatest impact (at home, on the road, in your car etc)

6. Discuss Information Resources, Inc – pg 608
This company provides data about advertising for various R&D professionals. Unfortunately, the information is of a general nature and does not specifically address itself to a particular product.

7. Discuss the marketing strategy of Pine-Sol – pg 610
Pine-Sol, a liquid cleaning agent, uses the sweepstakes method for a value-added sales promotion of its product. While occasionally successful if run ethically, sweepstakes promotions often run into problems of honesty. Even large companies like McDonalds and Burger King have had problems with this form of marketing.

8. Discuss the promotional tool for AKAI – pg 610
AKAI, a Japanese producer of electronics, uses trade-ins of old electronics as an incentive to buy its newer electronics. This strategy works well in India and Japan. The public feels that AKAI is foolishly overpaying for their used and often defective electronics, but the real strategy is to sell a new item. If the item's price is reduced by 20-25% by the trade-in, it is the same as having a sale plus they get to cash in the old electronics for parts and scrap metal. Not so foolish.

9. Discuss the marketing strategy of CoolSavings.com – pg 611
CoolSavings.com is exactly what its name says it is: Cool Savings. You go to the site for freeand print out coupons for free and redeem them at your local markets for savings. The brands of the coupons pay the site a penny for each coupon downloaded by a site visitor and everyone saves money.

Mark Zukerberg, founder of FACEBOOK

Internet Resources for this lesson:

General Reference Material For All Content

http://www.askmrmovies.com

Media Advertising
www.admedia.org/

How Facebook Succeeded

www.topclickmedia.co.uk

Tafero's Lesson Plan of Day
- Marketing Management -
Public Relations - Seventeen

Lesson 17 - Public Relations

The Bhopal Disaster was a PR nightmare

1. Discuss the variables of Public Relations****- pg 616
A. Press Relations – present news in a positive light (spin)
B. Product Publicity – Associate your product with a current event or figure
C. Corporate Communication – Internal and external data exchange
D. Lobbying – Government relations with legislators
E. Counseling – Free advice to the public and action during time of crisis

2. Discuss the marketing strategy of Brita – pg 617
Brita water filters promotes its brand in areas designated by good R&D that show a need for clean water. Very Clever.

3. Discuss the marketing strategy of Yahoo – pg 617
Yahoo nurtured PR far in advance of releasing its product on the internet. In six months, they had over 600 press coverage stories about Yahoo. An extremely successful media campaign and a good model to copy.

4. Discuss the marketing strategy of Random House – pg 619
The publisher Random House created a top 100 novel list of all time. Many disagreed with the list and it created controversy. Controversy sometimes is very good for new products and so Random House saw sales inadvertently climb. Some companies, such as supermarket rag magazines seek to create controversy intentionally to create sales. This is a double-edged sword. Controversy MAY increase sales, but it MAY also destroy the viability of your product. Be careful using this method.

5. Discuss the three new forms of mail which can be used for promoting products – pg 623
A. Email
B. Voice Mail
C. Mobil Phone Mail

6. Discuss the marketing strategy of Land's End – pg 626
Land's End is one of the best users of the catalog marketing strategy. This company even employed well-known writers to create stories around their products-a very creative and successful idea. The catalogue reads more like a magazine than a series of ads. A very good model for catalogues.

7. Discuss the marketing strategy of Eddie Bauer Inc. – pg 627
Eddie Bauer has taken the catalogue from the print medium into the internet with great success. You can actually dress up online in the clothes that Eddie Bauer

sells by using animation software. Very clever and very profitable and another good model to copy.

8. Discuss the marketing strategy of USAA – pg 628
One of the first insurance companies to take a customer from first call to writing a finished policy all in one call. This model later successfully copied by larger companies in this business such as Geico and Allstate.

9. Discuss the marketing strategy of First Direct (Midland Bank) – pg 628
This bank was the first to eliminate physical plants (marketplaces) and replace them with phone, fax and internet services (marketspaces) for at-home banking. Now copied by many major banks in the world such as Bank of America and others.

ICA Homework – Essays – Lesson Seventeen

If you can't see our ad clearly; you need more toxins!

Internet Resources for this lesson:

General Reference Material For All Content

http://www.askmrmovies.com

Public Relations

www.pr-squared.com/index.php/.../the-7-elements-of-good-pr

Bad PR

www.101publicrelations.com/.../when_pr_goes_really_bad_000194.htm

Tafero's Lesson Plan of Day - Marketing Management - Sales and Bargaining - Eighteen

Lesson 18 – Sales and Bargaining

Bargaining has been around since the dawn of man

1. Discuss the marketing strategy of Bethlehem Steel – pg 642
Bethlehem Steel cut expenses by reducing its sales force and creating a
marketspace online. The online site allows potential buyers to view, in detail, all of
the inventories available to them invisual form, which is superior to the verbal
approach of real-time salespeople. This strategy has increased profits at the same
time as it reduced expenses and is an excellent model to copy for sales.

2. What should be the goals of a sales training program**** - pg 645
A. Reps need to know and identify with the company
B. " " " " the company's products
C. " " " " the competition's products
D. " " " " their customers
E. " " " " how to make effective sales presentations
F. " " " understand field procedures and responsibilities

3. Discuss how IBM trains its sales people – pg 645
A. IBM uses high tech to train its sales people
B. The tech includes interactive role-playing videos

4. Discuss how Whirlpool trains its sales people – pg 645
A. Whirlpool actually sends its sales people to a farm for two weeks.
B. The farm is outfitted with Whirlpool products that the trainees must use every
day.

C. At the end of two weeks, the trainees know far more about the products than just taking classroom training.

5. Discuss how Owens-Corning trains its sales people – pg 647
A. Owens-Corning uses FAST, a stellar software product to train its reps
B. FAST utilizes data for presentations, product information and, most importantly, customer information including past purchases and other client history.

6. Discuss how Siebel Systems train its reps – pg 650
A. Siebel does not use the old-fashioned quota system.
B. Siebel measures customer satisfaction, repeat business and revenue as its prime indicators as to whether a sales person is succeeding.
C. This long-term approach creates greater sales stability for the company

7. Discuss the techniques of a good sales person****- pg 656
A. Overcoming Objections – resisting customer objections with a positive approach, asking for clarification, having the buyer answer their own objection, denying the validity of the objection or turn the objection into a reason for buying* (best)
B. Closing – techniques for closing include recognition of customer capitulation, suggest the A or B option, or use additional inducements such as a discount, gifts or extra product.
C. Follow-Up and Maintenance – customer satisfaction and repeat business are very important. The sales rep should make sure that all of the details of the sale are provided by company without any major changes (and no changes at all, if possible). The rep should make a follow-up call or visit after the product has been delivered and is in use to make sure the customer is satisfied. This should result in a future prospect for repeat business.

8. Discuss Classic Bargaining Techniques****-pg 659
A. Big Pot – leave yourself plenty of bargaining power by coming in high
B. Prestige Play – use someone with clout at your presentation
C. Well is Dry – make no more concessions
D. Check With the Boss – go through the process and say " Now I have to check with my boss"
E. Auction Method – If shopping around for the best price, let everyone know you are shopping around.
F. Divide and Conquer – Sell just ONE person at the presentation; they will sell the others.
G. Wet Noodle – do not say or do anything to indicate your position other than we will get back to you.
H. Be Patient – try to outwait your opponent
I. Split the Difference – suggest a compromise in the price that is still well in your profit range
J. Surprises – keep your opponent off-balance by changing your tactics from A-J.

Don't Insult Your Customers!

Write a paragraph on each of these essay questions:

1. Why are sales important to a company?
2. How can we learn to become good at sales on the internet?
3. How should we bargain?
4. How are sales related to our Strategic Plan?

Internet Resources for this lesson:

General Reference Material For All Content

http://www.easternstudiesdatabase.cn

Bargaining

www.gohongkong.about.com/od/.../a/bargaining_hk.htm

Good Sales Habits
www.ezinearticles.com

Tafero's Lesson Plan of Day - Marketing Management - Additional Issues of Marketing - Nineteen

1. Discuss trends in Company Organization**** – pg 666
A. Lateral Cooperation – more communication between departments
B. Outsourcing – reduce costs by cheap labor
C. Strategic Alliances – creating cost reducing partnerships
D. Flattening – reducing organizational levels
E. Focusing – choosing the most profitable businesses and customers
F. Empowerment – giving your personnel a sense of possibility

2. Discuss one of the marketing strategies of Campbell Soup – pg 669
Campbell soup uses segmentation to successfully market regional soups.

3. How should we go about organizing our Marketing Department? – pg 669
Laterally, a marketing department should contain the following: a marketing administrator, an advertising and sales promotionmanager, a sales manager, a Market R&D manager and a New Products manager

4. Discuss the marketing strategies of Kraft – pg 673
Kraft now actively seeks sales opportunities and improving efficiency as their main goals.

5. Discuss how to get R&D departments to better blend with the Marketing Department – pg 677
A. Joint seminars
B. Team up one of each department on a new product
C. Role Reversal period
D. Have a Third party be an unbiased adjudicator.

6. Discuss the role of creativity in marketing – pg 682
A. Make sure your marketing department is a blend of by-the-book and creative types

B. Use Brainstorming techniques
C. Be more observant
D. Get Feedback from others
E. Use outsourcing for creativity

7. Discuss some of the common faults of small companies**** – pg 684
A. Failure to set clear objectives and a system to measure progress
B. Failure to know profitability of each item sold in a company (Cost Accounting)
C. Failure to know the details of the competition
D. Failure to be timely in reports and R&D.

8. Discuss the very important variables of efficiency.**** – pg 694
A. Sales-Force Efficiency – ave number of calls per salesperson, time, revenue, cost, % of orders, total sales-force cost as % of total sales .
B. Advertising Efficiency – cost per 1000 buyers, consumer opinions of ads, cost per inquiry
C. Sales Promotion Efficiency - % of sales for each deal, display costs per sales dollar, % of coupons redeemed, number of inquiries per presentation
D. Distribution Efficiency – logistics cost as % of sales, % of orders filled correctly, % of on-time deliveries, number of billing errors.

Critical Questions

1. Discuss promotional efficiency.
2. Discuss advertising efficiency.
3. Discuss sales-force efficiency.
4. Discuss distribution efficiency.

Additional Internet Resources:
http://www.askmrmovies.com

Tafero's Lesson Plan of Day - Marketing Management - Conflict Resolution - Twenty

Lesson 20 – Conflict Resolution in Sales

The primary principles involved with conflict resolution arenegotiation, compromise, concession, advantage, disadvantage,and balance.

A. Negotiation – two or more parties must be willing to negotiate forthe purpose of achieving the other principles involved withnegotiation: compromise, making concessions, seeking advantages, accepting disadvantages and finding a balance within the negotiations. In the seller-buyer relationship, this translates into both sides realizing that there will be an exchange of more than just money for goods and services. Any number of variables can be negotiated in a contract scenario. All the variables are subject to the same principles that are involved in basic negotiation.

B. Compromise – In order for negotiations to be successful, both parties must be willing to compromise. Bad faith on the part of one or both parties not to compromise will result in a breakdown of negotiations. Both sellers and buyers need to adhere to this principle for a successful business arrangement that will stand the test of time.

C. Making Concessions- In negotiations, one must realize that one will be making one or more concessions. In return for a concession, one expects to gain one or more advantages and to lose one or more advantages. Concessions should be made in the spirit of balance. In the seller-buyer relationship, the most common form of concession is usually lowering the price in order to make a sale. But there are a myriad of other concessions both sides can agree to.

D. Advantage- both sides in negotiation will always seek to gain advantage over the other side. In negotiation, this must be done as subtly as possible with the impression there is no advantage at all for either side. A skilled negotiator will give the opposition the impression that the opposition has gained the advantage when, in fact, he or she has gained the advantage in the negotiation. This is actually a violation of good faith within negotiation and a very common outcome. In the long run, continually seeking advantage in negotiations might actually result in lower productivity by creating an adversarial relationship with your opponent rather than a relationship that fosters true compromise. In the buyer-seller relationship, this translates into giving the customer a fair return for the customer's money in order to maintain a long-lasting relationship.

E. Disadvantage – Both sides must realize there will be disadvantages as some point within thenegotiation. The obvious strategy is to gain as much advantage, while gaining the leastdisadvantage, but the obvious strategy is not always the best one. If one tries to give too muchdisadvantage to the other party, one violates the spirit of true negotiation and also endangers the MUTUAL advantage of a satisfying long-term relationship. This principle holds true for most governmental negotiations, business negotiations and personal negotiations with friends or the opposite sex. In the buyer-seller relationship, one must avoid giving too much disadvantage to the buyer, or the prospect of repeat business will be greatly diminished.

F. Balance – Both sides in a negotiation must seek balance. Only when a sense of balance is achieved by both sides will there be the possibility of agreement. Unbalanced negotiations will generally either fail in the short or long term. This relates to the buyer and seller as well in the form of gaining a short-term sale at the cost of a long-term customer when the price of an item does not provide long-term value to the customer. Generally speaking, the price of the item should reflect the length of long-term value to the customer; the higher the cost, the longer the item should perform at a quality level.

3. Premier Goal: Pg 15 – Discuss the Marketing Environment. Define Task Environment and its main actors as well as the Broad Environment and its components.

The Non-Profit Sector

A. Formulation of Non-Profits

B. Funding

C. Organization

D. Operation

Additional Internet Resource for Non-Profits

www.askmrmovies.com

www.ingramcontent.com/pod-product-compliance
Lightning Source LLC
Chambersburg PA
CBHW071723170526
45165CB00005B/2135